BEYOND THE
GASLIGHT

BEYOND THE
GASLIGHT

SCIENCE IN POPULAR FICTION 1895-1905

HILARY & DIK EVANS

With illustrations from the
MARY EVANS PICTURE LIBRARY

VANGUARD PRESS, INC.
424 Madison Avenue
New York, N.Y.

First published in Great Britain 1976 by Frederick Muller Ltd.
U.S.A. edition, 1977.

ISBN 0–8149 0782–2

The Vanguard Press, Inc.,
424 Madison Ave.,
New York, N.Y. 10017

Printed in Great Britain

CONTENTS

1 Peter Pan came from Outer Space

In the year 1900 everything suddenly seemed possible.

In this new century just dawning, surely men would fly. They could well fly to the moon. They might even travel back and forwards in time as well as this way and that in space.

When they had a continent to cross, they would travel by 200 mph monorail. When they had an ocean to cross, they would sail in giant passenger submarines, or they would travel beneath it in huge sub-oceanic pneumatic tubes linking one continent with another.

It was not only mechanical forces which twentieth century man would exploit. He would also tap the neglected powers within his own being — mesmerism, telepathy, animal magnetism — the latent faculties would be harnessed to accomplish feats dreamed of but never achieved by the visionaries of the past.

Wild speculation? Anything but. The citizen of 1900, looking forward with such high hopes to the century before him, based those hopes firmly on what had already been accomplished in the century behind him.

THE WORLD IN THE YEAR 2000
An enterprising French chocolate manufacturer of 1900 offered his customers a series of prophetic cards showing what life would be like at the close of the 20th century. Some of the predictions were absurd but many have been realised already.

Verne's 'Clipper of the Clouds' was not only an ingenious combination of ship and flying machine, but also used helicopter motors to provide lift.

For it had been a great century, no question of that. Back in 1800 there had been no railways, no steamships, no Suez Canal, no automobiles, no telephone or telegraph, no anaesthetics, no smooth roads, no way of recording sound, no electric light. The citizen of 1900 had all these at his command: he could look back over his shoulder with a gratifying sense of achievement.

Gratifying — but not satisfying. He wanted more and more. He hoped — he trusted — he *knew* — that the achievements of the nineteenth century were nothing to what would be achieved in the century just dawning.

An age of frenzied ventures

The foundations were already being laid. Take flying. Orville and Wilbur Wright in America, Hiram Maxim in Britain, Otto Lilienthal in Germany, not to mention thousands of like-minded enthusiasts in all parts of the world, were close to the secret of powered flight. Automobiles, some driven by steam or petrol and more advanced models powered by electricity, were driving the horse not only from the street but even from the sporting field, where cycle polo had threatened horse polo only to be ousted in its turn by motor polo. A Mr Halford had built the working model of a railway which would carry its passengers from London to Brighton, fifty miles, in fifteen minutes.

The planet itself was yielding the last of its secrets: the poles apart, little remained unmapped. And the poles themselves could not long hold out against such inspired onslaughts as those planned by Major Andrée (by balloon) or Mr Anderson (by sail-driven trailers on six-foot spherical wheels).

As for the forces inherent in man himself, their potential had been revealed by the sensational findings of the Society for Psychical Research's epoch-making *Phantasms of the Living* in 1886, and in other reports whose genuineness was vouched for by figures as respectable as Professor Gilbert Murray Ll.D., Litt.D., Professor William James, Professor of Psychology in Harvard University, or Sir William Crookes O.M., F.R.S. How could the citizen of 1900 doubt that it was only a matter of time before these wild talents, foreshadowed by Du Maurier in *Trilby* and Stevenson in *Dr Jekyll & Mr Hyde*, were tamed and set to work? Perhaps before the twentieth century was done with, telepathy would have rendered the telephone obsolete, while spirit travelling would have made the monorail and the sub-oceanic tube seem crude and cumbersome.

Mind you, there were disconcerting depths beneath the apparently respectable crust of the mind. The citizen of 1900 knew this because he had read Sigmund Freud's *Interpretation of Dreams*, appropriately published in the first year of the new century, almost as if intended as a warning. But then, every positive has its negative. Those who ventured

ALFORDS GRAVITY RAILWAY
Many inventors wanted to improve on existing railway technology — monorails, suspended tracks, atmospheric pneumatic propulsion and so on. Few were so daring as Alford's 'gravity railway' which, the inventor claimed, would carry travellers the 60 miles from London to Brighton in 15 minutes

to explore the mind of man were no more to be dissuaded by the thought that such knowledge might be dangerous than was Gottfried Daimler by the possibility that his horseless carriage might grow up to be a tank, or the Wright Brothers by the fear that a descendant of their fragile biplane might one day wipe out an entire city with a single bomb.

The citizen of 1900 could afford to be an optimist.

Waiting to applaud
Alas, however optimistic he might feel, however enthusiastically he might wish to hurry along this glorious future, the average citizen of 1900 had small chance of playing any personal part in the adventure. For every Orville Wright there were a million nameless bank clerks. For every Madame Curie, hundreds of millions of housewives and house-maids. For every Nansen who travelled to the Arctic, there were countless millions who never made a bolder voyage than the steamer trip down the Thames to Margate or up the Hudson to Poughkeepsie. Dentists and shopgirls, farmers and stockbrokers, their place in society was to keep society's wheels turning. Only at second hand could they share in the conquests which the pioneers made in their name.

When the pioneer triumphed, of course, the average citizen was on hand, waiting at the quayside or running alongside his carriage, cap in hand. But between triumphs, while the pioneer was making trial after painstaking trial, there was nothing the average citizen could do but wait.

Unless he happened to be a writer. Writers don't have to wait. No less fascinated than everyone else by the discoveries waiting round the corner, they could let their imaginations run on ahead and report what was in store for mankind.

Three thousand years of escapism
Man's oldest myths tell of never-never lands, sunset isles and halls fit for heroes: places where life is a sight happier, if generally less exciting, than it is in the here-and-now.

Our citizen of 1900 was living in the great age of anthropology, which had brought with it a new interest in mythology. His grandfather's age would have dismissed myth as crude tales fit only for peasants or children. The cuter stories — Cinderella and the Sleeping Beauty — were dressed up by dilettantes like Perrault to make pretty fairy tales: it wasn't till the more earnest Brothers Grimm set to work that the world began to see deeper meanings in these bedtime stories they had first heard at their nurse's knee. Baring-Gould's *Curious Myths of the Middle Ages* and Andrew Lang's *Myth, Ritual & Religion* helped people to look at the old stories with new eyes. Myth and symbol once again became living things. Wagner's *Ring of the Niebelung*, Maeterlinck's

'WHEN THE SLEEPER WAKES'
In Lanos, H. G. Wells for once found an illustrator with an imagination to match his own. His vision of a future civilisation is conceived on an appropriately colossal scale.

12

Blue Bird, Ibsen's *Peer Gynt* and Barrie's *Peter Pan* were among the consequences.

Certain themes have always fascinated man, whether or not he is aware of their deeper significance. The imaginary world, for instance. From classical Greece's Age of Gold to the Summerland of the Spiritualists, men have dreamed of fantasy worlds — and exploited them for every conceivable purpose. In the sixteenth century, when so many states were struggling towards nationhood, Thomas More's *Utopia* expressed his own ideal form of government — and a startlingly communistic government it was. A century later, in the age which saw the birth of modern scientific method, Bacon's *New Atlantis* preached experimental science as the only sound basis for a healthy society. Swift in the over-confident eighteenth century used his Lilliputians and Houynhmhnms to illustrate how ill-founded that self-confidence was.

The nineteenth century offered a wide choice of travel brochures for the world-weary armchair voyager. Bellamy's *Looking Backward* took him from the America of 1887 to that of 2000, by which time mankind has organised itself a little more intelligently — if somewhat socialistically. In *News from Nowhere* William Morris took him to a twenty-first century where the simple life has been re-established and the sun is always shining. Less complacently, Samuel Butler took him across the mountains to *Erewhon*, where he found a good many of his most cherished ideas turned upside down. And by the time W. H. Hudson depicted the *Crystal Age* into which his hero accidentally survives, the dream is beginning to turn into nightmare — a formula which Wells and his twentieth century followers were to exploit more deeply and more alarmingly.

Cardboard and Cavorite

Any writer who purports to describe an imaginary world must provide a certain amount of physical description — clothes, transport, houses, machines. Wells' readers want to know how the *First Men in the Moon* got away from the earth — so he satisfies them with Cavorite, a mysterious anti-gravitational substance. Past master of technological inventiveness was Jules Verne, whose range of devices is unequalled — from the rockets whereby *his* travellers got to the moon to the delightful plug-in cigar-smoking device described in *The Floating Island*. But for all his ingenuity, Verne's plots are crude and his characters cardboard. By and large his books were — still to a large extent are — regarded as fit only for children. A pity, because his was one of the most hard-working imaginations of the century. But the most satisfying writers in this field are those who could combine attention to detail with a broader, deeper vision.

'FROM THE EARTH TO THE MOON' Verne's prophetic account of the first moon-shot may have got a few details wrong, but got a great many more astonishingly right.

Bulwer Lytton was one of the most eminent pioneers of the Victorian occult movement, and his 'A Strange Story' eerily introduces black magic into the prosaic setting of an English country town.

Monsters in a cosy world

Take a world of antimacassars and aspidistras, as cosy as Trollope's Barchester or Elisabeth Gaskell's Cranford. Introduce a sinister Oriental versed in the ancient mysteries — and presto — you have a magic formula for fiction. Or so you'd think, but few Victorian writers realised it.

One of those few was Lord Lytton, better known for his big-screen spectaculars like *The Last Days of Pompeii*. He wrote a handful of tales concerned with the dark powers of the mind — the best of which, *Zanoni* and *A Strange Story*, describe the impact of a collision between the conventional everyday world and the unknown forces of the occult. Later, Du Maurier's strange *Trilby* and even stranger *Peter Ibbetson* presuppose the existence of supernormal mental powers — and take it for granted that their readers accept them too.

Which they would do, most of them, for the Magus is another of the eternally attractive myths — the man who by fair means or foul (usually foul: generally it involved selling his soul to the Devil) has got hold of esoteric knowledge which other men haven't got. This knowledge leads to power, though fortunately for mankind this power is seldom put to any more troublesome purpose than the seducing of a reluctant heroine. Mary Shelley's *Frankenstein* created the archetype of all monsters: William Godwin's *Caleb Williams* fled from a mysterious pursuer in an atmosphere of personal nightmare unequalled till Kafka.

The reader who had been brought up on such fare was ready to accept the occult as reasonable material for fiction, but of course, then as now, the mass of people didn't read books. However popular *Trilby* or *News from Nowhere* might be, they reached only a minority. It so happened,

ary Shelley's 'Frankenstein'
ust surely be the best-known
all horror stories, and its
ıality undoubtedly owes a
eat deal to her archetype of the
ientist obsessed by a single
m regardless of consequences.

however, that the rise of this type of imaginative fiction coincided with a trend so big that it constituted a cultural revolution in itself — the sudden and rapid growth of the illustrated magazine.

Words and pictures

Visualise a world without cinema or television, where most people had no access to picture galleries, where few books had illustrations except expensive volumes produced for the wealthy collector. You could admire the prints in the print-shop window, you could see crude woodcuts on ballad-sheets bought at the Fair, you might pore over the engravings in the family Bible and *Pilgrim's Progress* — and from these you had to form your ideas of the world beyond the horizon. No wonder if your notions of other lands were ludicrous caricatures.

It all changed in 1842 — when the greatest of all magazines, the *Illustrated London News*, first appeared. The imagination can work only if it has something to work with: it needs raw materials. A writer can tell of horrid spectres in haunted graveyards because his ingredients lie to hand. But till people had enlarged their experience with pictures such as those provided by the *Illustrated London News*, they could not travel far in their imaginations. It was no horror comic — nothing could be more pedestrian, in fact — but it encouraged people to use their imaginations. So it paved the way for later developments. Through the decades of the nineteenth century, magazines gradually evolved. From devotional periodicals intended to amuse and instruct on Sunday afternoons we move to sensational yarns for children in which schoolboys are forever running away to sea or setting up in business as frontiersmen in the Wild West. But it was only in the 1880s and 1890s that the true formula was reached — the popular monthly which revolutionised the reading habits of millions.

The *Strand Magazine* is generally given the credit for leading the revolution, though the *English Illustrated Magazine* had for a decade contained much the same blend of stories, articles and pictures. The *E.I.M.* appealed to a literate public: poems by Swinburne and Kipling alternate with stories by Hardy and Henry James; Bernard Shaw writes about Wagner, Oscar Wilde about the London scene, W. G. Grace about cricket and Robert Louis Stevenson about dogs.

The *Strand* aimed at a more popular audience. It had to — to sell profitably at sixpence, it needed a vast circulation. It achieved this by appealing to the most basic instincts of its readers. In its first issues they could read about cats, child workers in London, lost dogs, ladies' fashions, actors' dressing-rooms, opium dens. Success was immediate. The first issue sold 300,000 copies: the circulation rose to 500,000 and stayed there year after year. None of its rivals ever came near this figure.

But when those rivals appeared the *Strand* had to work harder to hold its readers. The most important change was on the fiction side: for the rest of their lives, the monthlies were locked in desperate battle to win and to hold the popular authors. The *Strand* would have led the field with Conan Doyle's Sherlock Holmes alone, but in addition it boasted W. W. Jacobs, immensely popular then if less so today, Kipling, and Wells whose *First Men in the Moon* it serialised. Conan Doyle got £30 a piece for his earlier Holmes stories, £50 later, and between £480 and £620 for the instalments of *The Hound of the Baskervilles*. Wells got about £80 a story.

In May 1893 Routledge's *Pall Mall Magazine* appeared, aimed at 'a high and refined literary and artistic standard' and priced at 1/- compared with the Strand's sixpence. There must have been a public willing to pay this, for though the *Pall Mall* never matched the circulation of the *Strand* it kept going for many years without lowering its standards. Contributors included Meredith and Hardy, Conan Doyle and Rider Haggard. It used Beardsley as an illustrator and published poetry by Kipling and Bret Harte, Swinburne and Verlaine (in French).

Ward Lock launched the *Windsor Magazine* in January 1895 as 'the biggest and best sixpennyworth ever issued'. It was not: it was bourgeois, pedestrian, unpalatable in appearance and uninteresting in content. Yet the *Windsor* is an example — surely unique in publishing history — of a magazine which improved with the years. In its first numbers we find articles on royalty, babies, cats and fashion: later came stories by Kipling and Arnold Bennett, Jack London and Jerome K. Jerome.

Pearsons Magazine with its delicious art nouveau cover appeared in January 1896. C. Arthur Pearson had no illusions about the risk he was taking: 'If it is not the best sixpennyworth that has been hitherto produced, it will be a failure. For unless it immediately attains, and succeeds in keeping, a colossal circulation, the enormous sum spent in producing each issue cannot possibly be justified.' But if the risks were high, so were the stakes: somehow, each newcomer found enough readers to keep going. It was some time before *Pearsons* could attract any really big names, but in their second volume they secured Wells' *In the Abyss*, and later came two serial scoops. Kipling's *Captains Courageous* and Wells' *War of the Worlds*. Thereafter, *Pearsons* was established as one of the most readable of the monthlies.

All these magazines had cost 6d or 1/-: in 1898 a newcomer appeared, only slightly thinner, for 3d: the *Harmsworth*. Its first editorial begins:—

OUR EXCUSE FOR THE ISSUE OF A SIXPENNY MAGAZINE AT THREEPENCE

The beginning of a new Magazine, once an event, is now so much a commonplace that the ancient excuse of the 'long felt want' no longer serves. The reader has of late years been harried by a direct, by an enfilading, and a ricochetting fire of new adventures, some honestly and avowedly frivolous, others portentously literary, a few loftily artistic. Every imaginable plan has been adopted whereby his capture might be affected. Projectiles calculated to vanquish by size and weight of paper have been hurled at him: there have even been surreptitious and spy-like attempts to enter his domestic circle by seeking the favour of his wives and daughters by means of 'Women's Departments', all frocks, furbelows and complexion cures: and worse, his very children have been attacked by page on page of 'Nursery Chat' and 'Tiny Tales for Little Listeners'.

He goes on to ask: 'Can such a publication as this be sold for 3d? Provided we reach a gigantic circulation, we can do it.' And he did it — partly by having slightly fewer pages than the others, partly by adopting a more lively (or more vulgar, depending on your viewpoint) layout, partly by not competing in the battle for big names. No Sherlock Holmes, no *War of the Worlds*. Yet even here the writer of imaginative fiction was represented.

All these magazines looked much the same — especially as no writer felt any tie of loyalty to an individual publisher, so that, for example, though the *Strand* serialised Wells' *First Men on the Moon*, his *War of the Worlds* was secured by *Pearsons* and *The Sleeper Awakes* by the weekly *Graphic*. Any of these monthlies — or any other of their lesser rivals, for we have named only the best-known — contains about 120 pages per issue. Most pages have pictures on them. There are two or three stories, illustrated features on animals, leading personalities, 'I Was There' articles. The respectably sensational is always prominent — nothing that might give offence, but sea-serpents and pirates, unusual cures and strange vehicles, detectives at work and disasters at sea.

As for the stories, they are nearly always variants on a boy-meets-girl theme, even when they purport to be detective stories or ghost stories or science stories. The action generally takes place in a higher social stratum than that of the average reader — most of the heroes in the stories we shall be considering seem to enjoy mysterious private incomes and live in vast houses with a staff of servants. Nor are the characters of the stories complex. Even where they have names, they seldom have individuality. For the most part they can be described in a single word — the Detective: the Colonel: the Explorer.

And, of course, the Scientist.

2 Science with the dessert course

If you'd asked the average citizen of 1900 what he understood by the word 'scientist', he'd have given you only the vaguest of answers. There was no such profession. No formal apprenticeship qualified you to become a scientist as you might become a doctor or a barrister. All you needed was the interest — and the money and the leisure to indulge that interest. And even the money was not frightfully important: the day had yet to come when scientific apparatus would cost astronomic sums beyond the reach of the private pocket — anyone could set up as a scientist with the barest of equipment.

The average adult of 1900 had not been taught any science worth mentioning at school: so he was in no position to criticise those who chose to set themselves up as experts. He was prepared to credit anything they told him — or alternatively, discredit everything — according to his cast of mind. On the whole, people inclined to belief in those days. There was so much happening in every scientific field — the internal combustion engine, electricity, wireless, X-rays, plastics, new fuels — and neither the scientist himself, far less the man in the street, could tell which of these would lead to valuable applications, which would turn out to be blind alleys.

The scientist was often described by the sonorous title of 'man of science'. Under this title the *Strand* published a long series of adventure stories. It was a fine-sounding title — but, like most fine-sounding titles, it didn't mean very much. It helped to be a doctor of something — it didn't much matter what — it helped, too, to have a German name. But basic equipment for setting up in business as a 'man of science' was no more than a perceptive mind and a desire to fill it with knowledge. If you didn't go about in blinkers as other people did, if you noticed things and wondered about them, why, you were a man of science! Take fossils — hundreds of people had seen them, some had even collected them as curios: but nobody regarded them as more than mere oddments in the ground until along came Mary Anning who saw what the others saw — and a little more. She saw, as they did, the bones of a fish in the rock: she knew, as the others did, that fishes don't swim in rocks: she sat down, as they had not, to think how these two facts could be reconciled. She was a scientist.

Many useful contributions to science were made by amateurs with private incomes who decided, after leaving the university, that life even in the Guards was too tiresome, the life of a man of letters too stultifying, the life of the politician too squalid, and so took up science instead. An attic or an outhouse would be converted into a laboratory. The family would be enlisted to help. Visitors would be invited to witness the experiments. Joseph Wright's splendid pictures, the *Experiment with an Air Pump* and *A Lesson in Astronomy*, date from an earlier age, but they illustrate beautifully the sense of personal involvement in science which today only the specialist can enjoy.

The apparatus used by the men of science matched this mood: it was designed to be looked at and admired, and was frequently beautiful in itself. The columns which supported the electric coils would be turned and polished rosewood, topped with little brass urns. Flasks would have elegant fluted stems: a brass bracket would be engraved with delicately swirling lines: graceful patterns would be etched onto a simple support.

Discoveries would be disseminated through the public lecture and the scientific conversazione, both of which were very popular activities. Every town of any consequence had its Philosophical and Scientific Society, at whose meetings members would read their papers and exhibit their finds. Eminent scientists like Faraday were expected, and glad, to give public lectures spreading the gospel of science to the public at large.

The *Analyst*, comparing the flesh-forming ingredients in Cocoas, gives the following average :—

" Flesh-forming ingredients in Natural Cocoa Nibs .. .. 18·00 "
"   ditto   ditto   in the best Commercial Cocoa with added Starch and Sugar   6·00 "
"   ditto   ditto   in Cadbury's Cocoa, the standard English article .. .. 21·00 "

" The process of preparation concentrates the nourishing and stimulating principles of the
Cocoa bean."

" Cadbury's Cocoa being Absolutely Pure is therefore the best Cocoa.

What was a scientific conversazione like? Conan Doyle gives us a delightful account of such a gathering in his *The Voice of Science:*—

'Mrs Esdaile, of Birchespool, was a lady of quite remarkable scientific attainments. As secretary of the ladies' branch of the local Eclectic Society she shone with a never failing brilliance. It was even whispered that on the occasion of Professor Tomlinson's suggestive lecture on The Perigenesis of the Plastidule, she was the only woman in the room who could follow the lecturer as far as the end of his title. There were bitter feminine whispers as to the cramming from Encyclopedias and text-books which preceded each learned meeting, and as to the care with which in her own house the conversation was artfully confined to those particular channels with which the hostess was familiar. So ran the gossip of the malicious, but those who knew her best were agreed that she was a charming and clever little person.

On her pleasant lawns in the summer, and round her drawing room fire in the winter, there was much high talk of microbes and leucocytes, and sterilised bacteria, where thin ascetic materialists from the University upheld the importance of this life against round comfortable champions of orthodoxy from the Cathedral Close. And in the heat and thrust and parry, when scientific proof ran full tilt against inflexible faith, a word from the clever widow would bring all back to harmony once more.

'A scientific conversazione in a private house is an onerous thing to organise, yet mother and daughter had not shrunk from the task. On the morning of the story they sat together, surveying their accomplished labours, with the pleasant feeling that nothing remained to be done save to receive the congratulations of their friends. They had assembled from all parts of Birchespool objects of scientific interest, which now adorned the long tables in the drawing room. Indeed the full tide of curiosities had overflowed the rooms devoted to the meeting and surged downstairs to invade the dining rooms and the passage. The whole villa had become a museum. Specimens of the fauna and flora of the Philippine Islands, a ten foot turtle carapace from the Gallapagos, the os frontis of the Bos Montis as shot by Captain Charles Beesly in the Thibetan Himalayas, the bacillus of Koch cultivated on gelatine – these and a thousand other such trophies adorned the tables upon which the two ladies gazed.'

The conversazione is merely the setting for the story. The curious may care to know that the plot concerns the daughter of the house, Rose, and the famous Captain Beesly who has proposed – and expects an answer today. Her brother Rupert knows him for the cad he is, but Rose will not listen. The high spot of the conversazione is a lecture given via the

A scientific conversazione as depicted by William McConnell n Sala's 'Twice Round the London Clock'.

phonograph — an early model which possessed a feature, not matched till the advent of the tape recorder, of being as easy to record as to reproduce. Rupert slips away and charges the machine with intimate details about the Captain's blackguardly conduct towards a Miss Lucy Araminta Pennyfeather and little Martha Hovedean of the Kensal Choir Union. Beesly ignominiously flees the house and Rose instead marries 'one of the most rising scientific men in the provinces'.

The Fairyland of Science

Those who were fathers in 1900 had enjoyed no formal scientific education, but they had had the opportunity to acquire a good deal of scientific knowledge. Innumerable textbooks must have been squeezed into innumerable Christmas stockings, by fond parents who hoped that their children would be both entertained and instructed by scientific facts elegantly set forth under such titles as *The Fairyland of Science* or *Madam How and Lady Why*. Many of these books were in dialogue form, and indicated the thirst for knowledge that the child was expected to display:

CHARLES: Father, you told Sister Emma and me that you would

explain to us some of the principles of natural philosophy. Will you begin this morning?

FATHER: Yes, I am quite at leisure: and I shall indeed at all times take a delight in communicating to you the elements of useful knowledge. These, I trust, will lead you insensibly to admire the wisdom and goodness by means of which the whole system of the universe is constructed and supported.

EMMA: But can philosophy be comprehended by children so young as we?

FATHER: Philosophy is a word which in its original sense signifies only a desire of wisdom: and you will not allow that you and your brother are too young to wish for knowledge.

CHARLES: So far from it, that the more knowledge I get the better I seem to like it.

Nor is Charles unique in his desire for scientific education: young James, from another book of the same type, is equally eager — and quick, too, at perceiving the role of science as an instrument of the divine purpose:

JAMES: Another beautiful evening presents itself; shall we take the advantage which it offers of going on with our astronomical lectures?

TUTOR: I have no objection, for we do not always enjoy such opportunities as the brightness of the present evening affords. And yet, divine wisdom and goodness apportions the quantity of light, according to the various Necessities of the inhabitants of the earth, in their different situations. Even at the poles, all the time that the sun is below the horizon, the moon never sets. And when the sun is depressed the lowest under the horizon, then the moon ascends with her highest altitude.

JAMES: This indeed exhibits in a high degree the attention of Providence to all his creatures.

More formal scientific education was gradually becoming available for the younger generation in 1900. Science was regarded as a valuable discipline: even, in the more advanced establishments, as being important in itself. There were separate lessons for the various branches — they were no longer all gathered together under the useful umbrella of 'natural philosophy' — and indeed science in 1900 covered a wider field than you might have thought. A magazine article in the 1890s speaks of 'an unique school for the training of female physical training teachers, where the subjects include eurhythmics, anatomy, hygiene, medical gymnastics, physiology and chemistry'. Christ's Hospital School had even innovated the heuristic method of teaching science, in which the pupil is encouraged to find things out for himself in his own way — a

LEARNING TO FLY IN 1955 No visionary of the future was more prolific than the French artist Robida, whose flights of fancy always took off from solid ground as in this 1892 prediction of a flying lesson of sixty years later.

A VICTORIAN FAMILY BEACHCOMBING Scientific research was something in which every member of the family could take part, and even a seaside walk — as this illustration from 'La Musée des Enfants' shows — could be a source of profitable instruction.

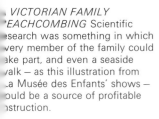

29

SCIENCE IN THE SCHOOLROOM The older educational establishments might stick to the classics, but science was infiltrating the state schools. This technical school at Finsbury featured in the 'Graphic', seems tolerably well equipped for 1884.

method which was discarded in the pursuit of factual knowledge, and which is only now being revived in the form of 'Nuffield' science.

In 1900, though, education hadn't reached the stage where children invariably seem to know more about the latest developments in science than their parents. Papa could still pontificate from the head of the dining table without derision from his progeny. And indeed the dining table provided a splendid theatre for his pontifications, for it afforded him all kinds of opportunities to demonstrate his familiarity with scientific principles. Nothing illustrates the Victorian attitude to science so well as the ingenuity with which scientific principles were demonstrated with domestic articles. After reading of experiments using forks, candles, wire from champagne corks, walnuts, soda syphons, wineglasses and all manner of crockery, one is tempted to think that the proper function of these implements was less as aids to eating than to provide the materials for a do-it-yourself lesson in science with the dessert course.

PARLOUR TRICKS Victorian fathers were fond of demonstrating the wonders of science to their admiring families, even though many a housewife must have feared for her furniture and best china.

Hard boiled egg, divested of its shell, passing through the neck of a glass bottle, under the influence of atmospheric pressure.

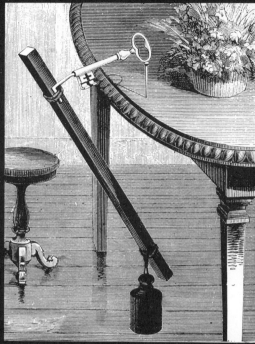

Balancing a weight on a nail and key.

E. PEUCHOT

A dry grape seed, when champagne is poured on it, will rise to the top with the bubbles, then sink then rise again.

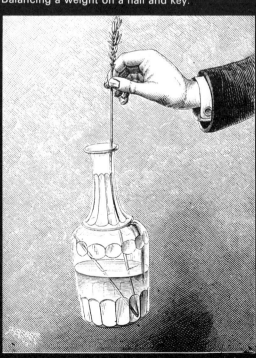

Lifting a bottle with a single straw.

Imagination unlimited

The children thus educated, who grew up to be the readers of the *Strand* and the *Windsor*, the *Pall Mall* and the *Harmsworth*, were naïve, ill-informed, but intensely curious about scientific matters. And the same goes for the writers who contributed to those magazines.

The fiction writers of the day seem to fall into two groups, when it comes to dealing with the world of science. On the one hand there were those who wanted to write about the new scientific discoveries, but felt obliged — or *were* obliged by their editors — to cram the science into a conventional boy-meets-girl framework. And on the other hand there were those who were perfectly happy to write conventional boy-meets-girl stories, but who felt obliged — or *were* obliged by imaginative editors — to insert a few fragments of science to pep the story up.

Either way, it is their gloriously unfettered imaginations which make them so fascinating to us today. It is not hard to picture how their

POWER FROM THE SUN
Nineteenth century technology started to explore many fields which remain uncharted even today. Pifre's power plant, which in 1882 successfully exploited solar energy to power a printing press, still represents a feasible possibility for our own power-hungry age.

stories might have been born. One evening a writer would be taken by a friend to a popular public lecture. The speaker, surrounded by gleaming equipment, demonstrates how with a curved glass the sun's rays can be intensified and enormous heat focussed onto a single spot. He winds up the lecture with some predictions about the possibilities of giant lenses, prophesying that some day cities will be heated by solar power, or armies frizzled by a weapon which gathers the sun's rays and directs them onto the chosen target in a concentrated death beam.

His imagination fired, our writer returns home. Before he falls asleep that night he recalls reading somewhere that a single drop of water will refract light to produce a rainbow, or can be used as a lens to focus light. His mind sets to work, combining the assorted ideas into a single whole . . . If one drop of water will do so much, what will not a million gallons do . . . a waterfall, say, curved like the Horseshoe Falls . . . a lens many feet across would be impossibly costly, but water costs nothing . . . such a fall would form a natural burning glass a hundred feet across . . . it would send a beam of scorching heat onto a certain spot . . . onto a rock, for instance, where the villain (and of course the

kidnapped heroine) is trapped . . . will the hero get there in time? And so a magazine story is born. Our hypothesis of how the story came into being is mere guesswork, but you can read the story itself in the *Strand* for May 1903.

In these magazines you come across many examples of stories in which writers seized hold of scientific ideas and stretched them far beyond any practicable lengths. At a conversazione like Mrs Esdaile's, some Man of Science would demonstrate Prince Rupert's Drops — little drops of molten glass allowed to cool rapidly by being dropped into water, setting up resultant strains which cause a small explosion when the end of the drop is crushed in a pair of pliers. Ooohs and aahs from the audience: but our writer is thinking how he can use this notion to titillate the readers of the *Strand* (September 1899). If this can be done with small drops of glass, then what can be done with larger drops . . . In fact, the principle applies to small drops only. Did the writer know better, was he having his readers on? Surely not. For the writer was no better informed than his readers: just a little more imaginative. Not a Man of Science, but another unquestioning worshipper.

'THE WAR OF THE WORLDS'
Though one of the leading
illustrators of the day, Warwick
Goble never did justice to Wells'
science fiction classic.

3 When the world froze

**Studies in disaster –
natural or man-made (and sometimes both)**

The Thames Valley Catastrophe (Grant Allen, 1897)

The Aerial Brickfield (John Mills, 1897)

A Corner in Lightning (George Griffith, 1898)

The River of Death (Fred M. White, 1904)

London's Danger (Cutcliffe Hyne, 1896)

'The Martians seem to have calculated their descent with amazing subtlety – their mathematical learning is evidently far in excess of ours – and to have carried out their preparations with a well-nigh perfect unanimity. Meanwhile the world went in ignorance of one of the gravest dangers that ever threatened the human race. It seems to me now incredibly wonderful that, with that swift fate hanging over us, men could go about their petty concerns as they did. For my own part, I was much occupied with learning to ride the bicycle. One night (the first Martian missile then could scarcely have been 10,000,000 miles away) I went for a walk with my wife. A party of excursionists from Isleworth passed us singing and playing music. From the railway station came the sound of shunting trains, softened almost into melody by the distance. It seemed so safe and tranquil . . .'

Man has always tormented himself with imaginary threats and calamities. It starts as fear – an atavistic wood-touching finger-crossing fear which insists that all pleasure is fleeting, that our apparent security is mere illusion. But how quick we are to turn even fear into pleasure! We have learnt to find a special enjoyment in being indoors on a stormy night, teasing ourselves with the possibility that our present happiness may vanish in a moment – while knowing full well that, with luck, it won't!

The Victorian age was one of peace and tranquillity for the average citizen, with just enough disasters – shipwrecks, volcanic eruptions, native uprisings in remote outposts of empire – to add spice to his morning paper. Seated comfortably in his commuter train, it was deliciously spine-tingling to lay the newspaper aside and take up a magazine containing fictional accounts of more spectacular disasters, reminding him how thin was the crust of safety over which his civilisation was advancing.

Nowhere was that crust apparently thicker than in London. There was the physical solidity of the great commercial buildings, the bridges and embankments, the great national monuments: and matching them was the moral stability of society, the conventions and observances of which, if they changed at all, changed only slowly, carrying the individual along on a reassuringly familiar ritual of accepted behaviour patterns.

But suppose those patterns were forcibly disrupted, those proud buildings levelled with the ground! Pride goes before a fall, and this vast man-made machine was the perfect example of what the Greeks called *hubris* – setting oneself above the gods: how could it long escape *nemesis*, the fate of Babel, the gods' punishment on overweening man! And so the overweening city clerk, as his train rattled towards the city, was warned how his city might any day be ravaged by French, German or Martian invaders: how minerals too recklessly mined could release unknown destructive forces: how his streets might be submerged by melting poles or buried beneath a flood of molten lava.

His train would draw into the terminus, he would tuck his magazine under his arm and hurry not to be late at his desk: but his head would still be ringing with the tocsin of alarm:

'In the hour of our pride we boasted that no nation on earth could lay us low. But the elements were set to war against our might, and they have humbled the British Empire even unto the ground.'

THE THAMES VALLEY CATASTROPHE

BY GRANT ALLEN.

IT can scarcely be necessary for me to mention, I suppose, that I was one of the earliest observers of the sad series of events which brought about the transference of the seat of Government in the British Isles from London to Manchester. My narrative naturally occupies a conspicuous position in the official report ordered by Parliament. But I think it incumbent upon me, for the benefit of posterity, to supplement that dry and formal statement by a more circumstantial account of my personal adventures, describing the great event as it appeared to myself, a Government servant of the second grade, and in its relations to my own wife, my home, and my children.

On the morning of the 21st of August, in the memorable year of the calamity, I happened to be at Cookham, a pleasant village which then occupied the western bank of the Thames just below the spot where the Look-Out Tower of the Earthquake & Eruption Department now dominates the whole wide plain of the Glassy Rock Desert.

In place of the black lake of basalt which young people see nowadays winding its solid bays in and out among the grassy downs, most men still living can well remember a gracious and smiling valley, threaded in the midst by a beautiful river.

I had cycled down from London the evening before and had spent the night at a tolerable inn in the village. Next morning I rose early, inflated my tyres, and set off towards Oxford by a leisurely route along the windings of the river. I began by crossing Cookham Bridge, which spanned the Thames close by the village: the curious will find its exact position marked in the maps of the period. In the middle of the bridge I paused and surveyed that charming prospect, which I was the last of living men to see as it then existed. I might have gazed at it too long – and one minute more would have sufficed for my destruction – had not a cry from the tow-path a little farther up attracted my attention. It was a wild, despairing cry, like that of a man being overpowered and murdered.

I am confident this was my first intimation of danger. Two minutes before, it is true, I had heard a faint sound like distant thunder: but nothing else. I turned my eye upstream. For half a second I was utterly bewildered. Strange to say, I did not first perceive the great flood of fire that was advancing towards me. I saw only the man who had shouted – a miserable, cowering, terror-stricken wretch, rushing wildly forward, with panic in his face as if pursued by some wild beast. 'A mad dog,' I said to myself, 'or else a bull in the meadow!'

I glanced back to see what his pursuer might be; and then, in a second, the whole horror of the catastrophe burst upon me. Its horror – but not yet its magnitude. I was aware at first just of a moving red wall, like dull red-hot molten metal. 'He must run,' I thought, 'or the moving wall will overtake him.' Next instant, a hot wave seemed to strike my face, like the blast of heat that strikes one in a glasshouse when you stand in front of the furnace. At about the same point in time I became aware that the dull red wall was really a wall of fire. But it was cooled by contact with the air and the water. Even as I looked, however, a second wave from behind seemed to rush on and break: it overlaid and out ran the first one. This second wave was white, not red – a white heat, I realised. Then, with a burst of recognition, I knew what it all meant – a volcanic fissure-eruption!

The poor wretch on the tow-path was not a hundred yards off – but as he rushed forwards and shrieked, the wall of fire overtook him. I do not think it quite caught him. It is hard at such moments to judge what really happens: but I believe I saw him shrivel like a moth in a flame a few seconds before the advancing wall of fire swept over him. He seemed to go off in gas, leaving a shower of powdery ash behind him. It is to this complete combustion before the lava-flood reached them that I attribute the circumstances that no casts of dead bodies, like those at Pompeii, have been found in the Thames Valley Desert. My own belief is that every human body was reduced to a gaseous condition by the terrific heat several seconds before the molten basalt reached it.

How high was the wall at that time? This has been much debated. I should guess thirty feet (though it rose afterwards to more than two hundred), and it advanced rather faster than a man could run down the centre of the valley. (Later on, its pace accelerated greatly with subsequent outbursts.)

In frantic haste, I saw that only one chance of safety lay before me: I must strike uphill by the field path to Hedsor. I rode for very life,

Next instant he shrivelled.

with grim death behind me. Even at this distance the heat was intolerable. Yet, strange to say, I saw few or no people flying as yet from the inundation. The fact is, the eruption came upon us so suddenly, so utterly without warning, that whole towns must have been destroyed before the inhabitants were aware that anything out of the common was happening. It is a sort of alleviation to the general horror to remember that a large proportion of the victims must have died without even knowing it; one second, they were laughing, talking, bargaining; the next, they were asphyxiated or reduced to ashes.

This, however, is what I learned afterward. At that moment I was only aware of a frantic pace uphill, over a rough stony road, and with my pedals working as I had never before worked them: while behind me I saw purgatory let loose, striving hard to overtake me. I just knew that a sea of fire was filling the valley from end to end, and that its heat scorched my face as I urged on my bicycle in abject terror.

All this time, I will admit, my panic was purely personal. I was too much engaged in the engrossing sense of my danger to be vividly alive to the public catastrophe. I did not even think of Ethel and the children. But when I reached Hedsor Church – whose shell still stands, scorched and charred, by the edge of the desert – I was able to pause for a minute to recover breath, and to look back on the scene of the disaster.

It was a terrible and yet I felt even then a beautiful sight. The whole valley was one sea of fire. Barriers of red-hot lava formed themselves for a moment now and again where the outer edge of the inundation had cooled a little: over these temporary dams fresh cataracts of white-hot material poured themselves afresh into the valley beyond. After a while, as the deeper portion of basalt was pushed out, all was white alike. So glorious it looked in the morning sunshine that one could hardly realise the appalling reality of that sea of molten gold.

I tried vaguely to discover the source of the disaster. Looking straight upstream past Marlow I described with dazzled eyes a whiter mass than any, glowing fiercely in the daylight like an electric light, and filling up the narrow gorge of the river towards Hurley and Henley. Though it was like looking at the sun, I could make out that the glowing white dome-shaped mass was the molten lava as it gurgled from the mouth of the vast fissure. I say vast, because so it seemed to me, though, as everybody now knows, the actual gap where the earth opened measures no more than eight miles across, from a point near what was once Shiplake Ferry to the site of the old lime-kilns at Marlow. Yet when one saw the eruption actually taking place, the colossal scale of it was what most appalled one.

I could see dimly, too, that the flood spread in every direction from its central point, both up and down the river. To right and left it was hemmed in by hills: but downward it had filled the entire valley as far as Cookham and beyond, while upward it spread in one vast glowing sheet towards Reading and beyond. I did not then know that this gigantic natural dam was later to fill up the whole low lying level and form the twin expanses of Lake Newbury and Lake Oxford. Tourists who now look down on still summer evenings where the ruins of Magdalen and Merton Colleges may be dimly descried through the pale green depths, their broken masonry picturesquely overgrown with tangled water-weeds, can form but little idea of the terrible scene which that peaceful bank presented while the incandescent lava was pouring forth in a scorching white flood towards the doomed district. It was with difficulty that I grasped my bicycle, my hands trembled so fiercely. I realised that I was a spectator of the greatest calamity which had befallen a civilised land within the ken of history.

As yet it did not occur to me that the catastrophe was anything more than a local flood. My imagination could hardly conceive that London itself was threatened. I thought at first 'It will go on towards Maidenhead!' But even as I thought it I saw a fresh and fiercer gush of fire well out from the central gash, and flow still faster down the valley. I realised with a throb that it was advancing towards Windsor. Then a wild fear thrilled through me. If Windsor, why not Staines and Chertsey and Hounslow? If Hounslow, why not London?

In a second I remembered Ethel and the children. Hitherto, the immediate danger of my own position alone had struck me. The fire was so near; the heat of it rose up in my face and daunted me. But now I felt I must make a wild dash to warn – not London – no, frankly, I forgot those millions; but Ethel and my little ones. In that thought, for the first moment, the real vastness of the catastrophe came home to me. The Thames Valley was doomed! I must ride for dear life if I wished to save my wife and children!

I mounted again, but found my shaking feet could hardly work the pedals. My legs were one jelly. With a frantic effort, I struck off inland in the direction of Burnham: I hardly knew the district well enough to know what route I must take in order to avoid the flood of fire. By pure instinct, I set my face Londonwards along the ridge of the chalk downs. In three minutes I had lost sight of the burning flood, and was deep among green lanes and under shadowy beeches. The very contrast frightened me. I wondered if I was going mad. It was all so quiet. One could not believe that scarce five miles from that devastating sheet of fire, birds were singing in the sky and men toiling in the fields as if nothing had happened.

Near Lambourne Wood I met a brother cyclist, just about to descend the hill. A curve in the road hid the valley from him. I shouted aloud: 'For heaven's sake, don't go down! There is danger, danger!'

'I can take any hill in England!' he answered.

'It's not the hill. There's been a volcanic eruption – great floods of fire – all the valley is filled with burning lava!'

'Go home to your lunatic asylum!' he cried derisively, pedalling faster down the hill. I have no doubt he must have ridden into the very midst of the flood and been scorched by its advance before he could check his machine on so sudden a slope.

I rode on at full speed among green fields and meadows. Here and there I passed a labouring man on the road. More than one looked up at me and commented on the oppressive heat, but none of them seemed to be aware of the fate that was overtaking their own homes close by in the valley. I told one or two, but they laughed as if I were a madman. I grew sick of warning them.

On the edge of the down, near Burnham, I caught sight of the valley again. Here, people were just waking to what was taking place. Half the population was gathered on the slope, looking down with wonder on the flood of fire. Silent terror was the prevailing expression. But when I told them I had seen the lava bursting forth from the earth in a white dome, they laughed me to scorn: and when I assured them I was pushing forward in hot haste to London, they answered 'It won't ever get as far as London!' That was the only place, as is now well known, where the flood was observed long enough beforehand to telegraph and warn the inhabitants of the great city; but nobody thought of doing it; and I must say, even if they had done so, there is not the slightest probability that the warning would have attracted the least attention. Men on the Stock Exchange would have made jests about it – and proceeded to buy and sell as usual.

Looking down from the hill toward the main road which runs along the Thames Valley towards London, I became aware that it was already crowded with carriages, carts and cycles, all dashing at a mad pace unanimously towards London. Suddenly a fresh wave turned the corner by Maidenhead Bridge, and began to gain on them visibly. It was an awful sight. I cannot pretend to describe it. The poor creatures on the road rushed wildly, despairingly on: the fire took them from behind and, one by one, before the actual sea reached them, I saw them shrivel and melt away in the fierce white heat. I could not look at it any longer. I certainly could not descend and court instant death. I felt that my one chance was to strike across the downs and try the line of northern heights to London.

Oh, how fiercely I pedalled! At Farnham Royal (where again nobody seemed to be aware what was happening) a policeman tried to stop me for frantic riding. I tripped him up and rode on. Experience had taught me that it was no use telling those who had not seen it of the disaster. A little beyond, at the entrance to a fine park, a gatekeeper tried to shut a gate in my face, exclaiming that the road was private. I saw it was my only practicable route, and this was no time for trifling. I am a man of peace, but I lifted my fist and planted it between his eyes. Before he could recover from his astonishment, I had mounted again and ridden on.

At Galley Hill I realised that my only hope lay in crossing the Valley at Uxbridge in order to gain the higher ground beyond. But could I cross before the lava-flood reached this point? Not far behind me, over the valley, hung a great white cloud – the steam of the river, where the lava sucked it up and made it seethe and boil. The flood was fast advancing. But in a second I realised I had no choice: I made up my mind to descend and cut across the low-lying ground. If I failed, after all, I was but one unit more in the prodigious calamity.

I was just coasting down the hill, when a slight and unimportant accident almost rendered impossible my further progress. I was pulled up suddenly by finding my front tyre deflated – I had received

The poor creatures rushed wildly,
despairingly on.

43

a bad puncture from a thorn on the road. I tried inflating again, but it was quite useless: I must submit to stop and doctor up the puncture. Fortunately, I had the necessary apparatus in my wallet.

I think it was the weirdest episode of all that weird ride – stopping impatiently while the fiery flood surged on, going through all the fiddling details of mending a pneumatic tyre. A countryman in a cart came past, saw me struggling frantically, and said 'The more haste the less speed!'

Should I warn him of his doom? 'Keep up on the hills!' I told him. 'Flames of fire are flowing down the valley.'

He burst into a laugh. 'Why, you're one of those Salvation Army fellows, trying to preach to me! I'm going to Uxbridge.' And he continued down the hill towards certain destruction.

It was hours, I feel sure, before I had patched up that puncture, though I did it by the watch in four and a half minutes. As soon as it was done I mounted once more and rode at a breakneck pace to Uxbridge and swept through the straggling main street. Nobody took the slightest heed; they stood still in the street for a moment watching me pass, then returned to their customary occupations. A quarter of an hour later there was no such place in the world as Uxbridge.

I rode on through Harrow without one word to anybody – partly because I did not desire to be treated as an escaped lunatic, partly because I rightly judged that they were safe from the inundation: for, as the flood never quite covered the dome of St. Paul's, part of which still protrudes from the sea of basalt, it did not reach the level of Harrow and the other northern heights of London. At Willesden I found great crowds of people in the profoundest excitement watching a dense cloud of smoke and steam that spread rapidly from the west. They were speculating as to its meaning, but laughed incredulously when I told them what it portended. A few minutes later the smoke spread ominously towards Kensington and Paddington. That settled my fate. It was clearly impossible to descend into London: and indeed, the heat now began to be unendurable. It drove us all back, almost physically. I thought I must abandon all hope. I should never even know what had become of Ethel and the children.

My first impulse was to lie down and await the fire-flood. Yet the sense of the greatness of the catastrophe seemed somehow to blunt one's own private grief. I was beside myself with fear for my darlings; yet I realised I was but one among hundreds of thousands of fathers in the same position. What was happening at that moment in the great city of five million souls we did not know, we never shall know; but we may conjecture that the end was mercifully too swift to entail much suffering.

All at once a gleam of hope struck me. It was my father's birthday. Was it not just possible that Ethel had taken the children to Hampstead to wish their grandpapa many happy returns of the day? With a wild determination not to give up all for lost, I turned my front wheel in the direction of Hampstead Hill. My heart was on fire within me. A restless anxiety urged me to ride my hardest, as all along the route I was still just a minute or two in front of the catastrophe. People were beginning to be aware that something was taking place – more than one asked me eagerly where the fire was. It was impossible to believe they knew nothing of an event I seemed to have been living with for months: how could I realise that all the things had happened since I started from Cookham Bridge were really compressed into the space of a single morning – nay, more, of an hour and a half only?

I pedalled on as if automatically: for all life had gone out of me. I approached Windmill Hill: my heart stood still. At my father's door I drew up, hardly daring to go in. Though each second was precious, I still hesitated.

At last I turned the handle. I heard somebody within. It was little Bertie's voice. 'Mammy, Mammy, Daddy has come home!'

I flung myself into a chair and broke down. In that moment of relief, I felt that London was lost, but I had saved my wife and children. I did not wait for explanations. A crawling four-wheeler cab was loitering by. I hailed it, and hurried them in. I gave the driver three pounds – all the gold I had with me. 'Drive on, towards Hatfield – anywhere!' I cried.

He drove as he was bid. We spent that night, while Hampstead flared like a beacon, at an isolated farmhouse on the high ground in Hertfordshire. For of course, though the flood did not reach so high, it set fire to everything inflammable in its neighbourhood.

Next day, all the world knew the magnitude of the disaster. It can only be summed up in five emphatic words: there was no more London.

THE AERIAL BRICKFIELD

by JOHN MILLS

GEORGE Stanford was a genius in his way, and had ideas. It is to trace the development of one of his ideas that I pen these lines. He was a man of unusually large pecuniary resources, who spent his time and substance, and amused himself at the same time, in all sorts of odd schemes for increasing his wealth. And if it sometimes turned out that the emoluments were a negative quantity, such losses were nothing to him compared with one or two tremendously big hits which he made during his lifetime.

It was of one of these that he chose to tell me one night, sitting in the smoking room of his house, seated in contented silence before a small table on which were glasses and decanters. 'Make yourself comfortable,' he said suddenly, 'and I'll tell you a story embodying one of the most remarkable incidents of my life.' Do you happen to know Pictet, of Geneva, and Cailletet, of Paris?'

'Never even heard their names before!'

'Ah, I forgot you don't dabble in chemistry. Pity! Well, those two foreigners have demonstrated how to transform the air we breathe

into a liquid and even a solid on a small scale. But so far as I know
they never made any practical use of it. Well, when I first heard the
news – it is a long time ago now – I at once began to con over in my
mind ways and means for doing on a large scale – by the ton in fact –
what these men had done by the fraction of an ounce, and I succeeded
even beyond my most sanguine expectations. As a matter of fact I
manufactured solid air, as ice is made commercially, and I turned it
out in quantities such as Pictet and Cailletet never dreamed of.

'It was pretty plain sailing for certain adaptations of the solid air
in place of ice – for of course solid air is very cold, about 140 degrees
below that of ice. So I had it moulded into small pellets as a cooler
for drinks – instead of having your tumbler half filled with ice you
put in a pellet of solid air. Then again, I thought, it would be a great
convenience to millions of people to have a seaside atmosphere

packed up and brought to their homes by parcel post. You might have air from the sunny South, from any climate whatever, charged with varying proportions of ozone, for the use of invalids. And so on, and so on. But curiously enough, the most extraordinary idea was forced upon me one day without any effort on my part. You see, it suddenly struck me that my machine delivered the solid mass of air in the form of an elongated rectangular shape – for all the world, the shape of a brick.

'It was then that I thought I saw a big fortune looking in at the door. I saw that there would be little expense, comparatively speaking, in the plant; nothing but a powerful engine to work the pumps, and the bricks could be pushed out *ad infinitum*. Of course, something had to be done before those bricks could be of any use as building material. In the first place they were so cold that they burnt you like red-hot iron when you touched them. Again, the bricks took a fancy to the habit of growing beautifully less and melting into the atmosphere, passing up before my eyes like mist before the rising sun.

'Awkward indeed – but I got over it. I found a substance, which I named ''bindene'', which, when dissolved in water, possessed the properties of cement in the highest degree. When my air-bricks were immersed in this solution they became as hard as adamant. The constituent molecules were so firmly locked together by the bindene that restoration to normal temperature didn't affect the bricks in the least.

'When I found that I – one man, one machine, you know – could manufacture 30,000 air-bricks in the course of a 10-hour day, that I could teach the most unsophisticated to work the machine, and that there was practically an unlimited source of material gratis and always ready to hand, I began to view the invention as a thing of the highest commercial importance. For a while I turned the bricks out at a great rate. You see I had the field all to myself, and my point was to make a large quantity before the invention became known. So I went in for quantity and made millions – and mind you, there's a lot of air in an air-brick.

'And then I had to stop. I found that in the interests of humanity it was my duty to forego that source of income.

'It came to me only gradually. There was a very heavy rainfall that year, which proved most disastrous to the crops, ruined hundreds of farmers, and filled the newspapers with mournful prognostications for the future. Some attributed the excessive deluge to the large number of spots on the sun. I was never much of a believer in the influence of sun-spots on our weather, and amused my mind by speculating on a more likely cause. I began to note the daily barometric readings to see if they suggested any pattern – and found, to my amazement, that the daily fall of the barometer was exactly in proportion to the number of bricks that I had made. It dawned upon me that I was the unconscious agent of all the distress

dropped down just where I
as.

of that unhappy period! You see, the vast quantities of air that I was removing from the atmosphere were appreciably altering the weight of the entire envelope of air round the globe. In time the air had become so thin and attenuated that it wouldn't hold up the watery vapour, which consequently came down as a deluge of rain and ruined all those poor families.

'What could I do? I had no choice. I stopped the machine forthwith and set about devising some means for the restoration of the air to its normal condition. But I was thwarted by my own ingenuity. The bindene had imparted a hardness to the air-bricks which stubbornly resisted all attempts at turning them back again into air. I tried all sorts of solvents – acids and alkalis and I don't know what – but they failed utterly. Then I tried heating the bricks in a furnace, but they came out like red-hot blocks of iron, totally unchanged. What was I to do? I was at my wit's end when suddenly an idea came. I made a strong solution of the bindene, and to my intense relief I found that an air-brick, after soaking in this strong solution, lost the adhesive property the bindene had given it.

'Then nothing remained, but to dissipate the air as quickly as possible. I tucked up my sleeves to the work in earnest. Of course, after soaking – no mean task, bear in mind – the bricks began at once to evaporate; but to expedite the process I placed the bricks in a furnace, from which they disappeared like melting snowflakes, keeping up a regular roar like a whirlwind all the time. As I didn't care to let people know what I was about, I kept the affair to myself: I worked at that furnace day and night for weeks, snatching a few hours' sleep at intervals when I could hold out no longer. I can't tell you the pleasure I felt as I saw the barometer rise day by day. Up it went as the piles of bricks diminished. When the last brick was placed in the furnace I dropped down just where I was in complete exhaustion and slept for I know not how long. After that there was no more rain to speak of for three whole months.'

'You saved the crops, then?'

'No, but I saved the world. You see, had I continued making the bricks on the scale I planned, you will readily see that in no great length of time the air would have become so thin that no one could have breathed with comfort, and thus the human race would have been slowly exterminated.'

by GEORGE GRIFFITH

INNER was over. The coffee service and the liqueur case were on the table, and Mr Sidney Calvert, a well set-up young fellow of about thirty, was walking up and down on the opposite side of the table smoking a cigarette. Mrs Calvert, in the depths of a big cosy armchair beside the fireplace, had just emptied her coffee cup.

'Really, Sid, I must say that I can't see why you should do it. Of course it's a very splendid scheme and all that sort of thing, but surely you, one of the richest men in London, are rich enough to do without it. I'm sure it's wrong, too. What should we think if somebody managed to bottle up the atmosphere and made us pay for every breath we drew? Besides, how are you going to get to the Pole, to put up your works?'

'Well, in the first place, as to the geography, I must remind you that the Magnetic Pole is not the North Pole. It's in Boothia Land, British North America, some 1500 miles south of the Pole. As to the rest, it would be impossible to run any business and make money out of it on the lines of the Sermon on the Mount. When they find that cables and telephones and telegraphs won't work, and that no amount of steam-engine grinding can get up a respectable amount of electric light – when, in short, all the electric plant of the world loses its value, and can't be set going without buying supplies from the Magnetic Polar Storage Company, or, in other words, from your humble servant and the few friends that he will be graciously pleased to let in on the ground floor – well, it becomes a simple business transaction. Nothing "wrong" about that. Besides, no reason why we shouldn't improve the quality of the commodity. "Our Extra Special Refined Lightning!" "Our Triple Concentrated Essence of Electric Fluid!" – look very nice in advertisements, wouldn't it?'

'Don't you think that's rather a rivolous way of talking about a scheme which might end in ruining one of the most important industries in the world?' she asked, but before her husband could answer there was the sound of the doorbell.

Professor Kenyon.

'That's the Professor, I expect.'

'Shall I go?'

'Certainly not – unless you think the scientific details will bore you.'

'Oh no, they won't do that. Ah, good evening, Professor,' she exclaimed, as the man of science was admitted by the manservant.

'My wife and I were just discussing the ethics of this storage scheme,' Sidney Calvert explained.

'I think it will be a very wicked scheme if it succeeds, and a very foolish and expensive one if it fails,' she added.

'The ethics of the matter are no business of mine, nor have I anything to do with its commercial bearings,' the Professor replied. 'You have asked me merely to look at technical possibilities and scientific probabilities, and I don't propose to go beyond those. I've had a long talk with Markovitch this afternoon: I never met a man

52

who knew as much about magnetism and electricity. His theory that they are the celestial and terrestial manifestations of the same force, and that what is popularly called electric fluid is developed only at the stage where they become one, is itself a stroke of genius. His idea of locating the storage works over the Magnetic Pole of the earth is another, and I am bound to confess that, subject to one or two reservations, he will be able to do what he contemplates.'

'And the reservations – what are they?'

'First, that in all untried schemes of this sort, something utterly impossible to foresee may happen – and there you are, left in the lurch, your enterprise ruined. And second, it may be very dangerous for those engaged in the work.'

'Any more?'

'Yes, a warning, Mr Calvert. You propose to interfere very seriously with one of the subtlest and least-known forces of Nature. The consequences might be most disastrous, not only for those engaged in the work, but even the whole hemisphere, and possibly the entire planet.'

'Well, I think that quite good enough to gamble on, Professor.' Calvert was thoroughly fascinated by the grandeur of his scheme. 'I am much obliged to you for putting it so clearly. Unless something unexpected happens, we shall get to work on it at once. Just fancy what a glorious thing it will be to play Jove to the nations of the earth, and dole out lightning to them at so much a flash!'

*   *   *

A little more than a year had passed. During that time the preparations for the great experiment had been swiftly but secretly carried out. Ship after ship loaded with machinery, fuel and provisions, and carrying labourers and artificers to the number of some hundreds, had sailed away into the Atlantic. Mr Calvert himself had disappeared two or three times, and neither admitted nor denied the various rumours which got into circulation in the City and the Press.

Some said it was an expedition to the Pole, and that the machinery consisted of ice-breakers and steam sledges which were to attack the ice-hummocks like battering rams, and so smooth a road to the Pole. Others declared that the object was to plough out the North-West Passage and keep a waterway from Hudson's Bay to the Pacific open all year round. So well had the precautions been taken that not even a suspicion of the true object of the expedition had got outside the little circle of those who were in his confidence.

So far everything had gone as Orloff Markovitch, the Russian Pole to whose genius the inception of the gigantic project was due, had predicted. He himself was in supreme control of the costly works which had grown up under his supervision on that lonely spot in the far North where the magnetic needle points straight down to the centre of the planet.

Professor Kenyon had paid a couple of visits with Calvert. So far not the slightest hitch or accident had occurred, and nothing abnormal had been noticed in connection with the earth's electrical phenomena save unusually frequent appearances of the Aurora Borealis, and a singular decrease in the deviation of the mariner's compass. Nevertheless the Professor had firmly refused to remain until the gigantic apparatus was set to work: he and Calvert had come back to England just before the initial experiment was to be begun.

The 20th of March, the day fixed for the commencement of operations, came and went, to Mrs Calvert's intense relief, without anything out of the common happening. Though she knew that over a hundred thousand pounds of her husband's money had been sunk, she found it impossible not to feel a thrill of satisfaction in the hope that Markovitch had made his experiment and failed. She had escaped from the rigours of an English spring to a villa near Nice, where she was awaiting the arrival of her second baby. Calvert himself, busy with the home details of his scheme, could run over to Nice only now and then.

It so happened that Miss Calvert put in an appearance a few days before she was expected. Her mother sent a maid to inform Sidney Calvert of the fact by telegram, asking him to come over at once. In about half-an-hour the maid came back with the form in her hand: in consequence of some accident, the wires had ceased to work properly and no messages could be got through.

At first Kate Calvert could not understand – and then she understood only too well. The experiment had been a success after all! Markovitch's mysterious engines had been all the time inperceptibly draining the earth of its electric fluid and storing it up in the vast accumulators which would only yield it back again at the bidding of the Trust which was controlled by her husband!

When it got dusk that night, and the electric lights were turned on, it was noticed that they gave an unusually dim and wavering light. By midnight, all telegraphic and telephonic communication north of the Equator had ceased, and the electricians of Europe and America were at their wits' end. Next morning it was found that, so far as all the marvels of electrical science were concerned, the world had gone back a hundred years. Civilised mankind had been suddenly deprived of an obedient slave which it had come to look upon as indispensable.

But there was something even more serious to come. A remarkable drought had set in almost universally. A strange sickness, beginning with physical lassitude and depression of spirits which confounded the best medical science of the world, was manifesting itself far and wide, and rapidly assuming the proportions of a gigantic epidemic.

In the physical world, too, metals were found to be affected. Machinery of all sorts got 'sick': forges and foundries came to a standstill for the simple reason that metals seemed to have lost their best properties. Railway accidents and breakdowns on steamers became matters of everyday occurrence, for piston rods and propellor shafts had acquired an incomprehensible brittleness which only began to be understood when it was discovered that the electrical properties which iron and steel had formerly possessed had almost entirely disappeared!

So far Calvert had not wavered in his determination. To him, these calamities were only so many arguments for the ultimate success of his scheme – proof positive that the Calvert Storage Trust really did control the electricity of the world. It was now getting towards the end of May. On the 1st of June Markovitch would stop his engines and permit the vast accumulation of electric fluid to flow back into its accustomed channels. Then the Trust would issue its prospectus, setting forth the terms on which it was prepared to permit the nations to enjoy this gift of Nature.

On the evening of May 25th Calvert was sitting in his sumptuous office in Victoria Street, writing by the light of a dozen wax candles in silver candelabra. He had just finished a letter to his wife, telling her to keep her spirits up: in a few days the experiment would be over and everything restored to its former condition, after which she would be the wife of a man who would be able to buy up all other millionaires in the world.

As he put the letter into its envelope there was a knock at the door, and Professor Kenyon was announced. Calvert greeted him coldly, for he more than half guessed the errand he had come on. 'It's no use, Professor. You know yourself that I am as powerless as you are. I have no means of communicating with Markovitch: the work cannot be stopped before the appointed time.'

'I have kept your criminal secret too long, and I will keep it no longer. You have made yourself the enemy of Society, and Society has still the power to deal with you . . .'

'That's nonsense, and you know it! If Society were to lock me up, it would not get its electricity except on Markovitch's terms, which would be higher than mine. Tell your story whenever you please – it will neither stop our plan nor benefit Society!'

Baffled, the Professor was about to leave when the door opened and a boy brought in an envelope deeply edged with black. Calvert turned white to the lips, and his hand trembled as he opened it. It was in his wife's handwriting, and was dated five days before, as most of the journey had to be made on horseback. He read it through with fixed, staring eyes, then he crushed it into his pocket and strode towards the telephone. He rang the bell furiously, then remembered that he had made it useless. He opened the door and shouted for a clerk. 'Get me a hansom at once!'

'What is the matter, where are you going?' asked the Professor.

'Matter? Read that! My little girl is dead – dead of that accursed sickness which I have brought on the world. My wife is down with it too, and may be dead by this time. My God, what have I done?

Curse Markovitch and his infernal scheme! If she dies I'll go to Boothia Land and kill him! Hullo! What's this – lightning? Thunder!'

As he spoke, such a flash of lightning as had never split the skies of London before flared in a huge ragged stream of flame across the zenith, and a roar of thunder such as London's ears had never heard shook every house in the vast city to its foundation. Another and another followed in rapid succession, and all through the night and well into the next day there raged, as it was afterwards found, almost all over the whole Northern hemisphere, such a thunderstorm as had never been known in the world before and never would be again.

With it, too, came hurricanes and deluges of rain: and when, after raging for nearly 24 hours, it at length ceased convulsing the atmosphere and growled itself into silence, the first fact that came out of the chaos was that the normal electrical conditions of the world had been restored – after which mankind set itself to repair the damage done by the cataclysm and went about its business in the usual way.

The epidemic vanished instantly and Mrs Calvert did not die. Nearly six months later a white-haired wreck of a man crawled into her husband's office and said feebly: 'Don't you know me, Mr Calvert? I'm Markovitch, or what's left of him.'

'Good heavens! What has happened to you? Sit down and tell me about it!'

'It is not a long story, but it is very bad,' said Markovitch in a thin, trembling voice. 'Everything went well at first. All succeeded as I said it would. And then, just four days before we should have stopped, it happened. We must have gone too far, or some accidental discharge must have taken place. The whole works suddenly burst into white flame. Everything made of metal melted like tallow. Every man in the works died instantly, burnt to a cinder. I was four or five miles away with some others, seal shooting. We were all struck down insensible. When I came to myself I found I was the only one alive. Yes, Mr Calvert, I am the only man who has returned from Boothia alive. The works are gone. There are only some heaps of melted metal lying about on the ice. After that I don't know what happened. I must have gone mad. Some Eskimos found me wandering about, and they took me to the coast. Then I was picked up by a whaler and so I got home. That is all.'

His face fell forward into his trembling hands, and Calvert saw tears trickling between his fingers. Then he reeled backwards, and suddenly his body slipped gently out of the chair and onto the floor. When Calvert tried to pick him up he was dead. And so the secret of the Great Experiment, so far as the world at large was concerned, never got beyond the walls of Mr Sidney Calvert's cosy dining-room after all.

The whole works suddenly burst into white flame.

THE RIVER
OF DEATH

by FRED M. WHITE

THE sky was as brass, a stifling heat radiated from stone and wood and iron – a close, reeking heat that drove one back from the very mention of food. The five million odd people that go to make up London, even in the cream of the holiday season, panted and gasped and prayed for the rain that never came. For the first three weeks in August the furnace fires of the sun poured down till every building became a vapour bath with no suspicion of a breeze to temper the fierceness of it. Even the cheap press had given up sunstroke statistics.

The drought had lasted since April. Tales came up from the provinces of stagnant rivers and quick, fell spurts of zymotic diseases. For some time the London water companies had restricted supplies, but there was no suggestion of alarm. The heat was almost unbearable but, people said, the wave must break soon and the metropolis would breathe again.

Professor Owen Darbyshire crawled homewards towards Harley Street with his hat in his hand, his grey frock coat showing a wide expanse of white shirt below. There was a buzz of electric fans in the hall, yet the atmosphere was hot and heavy. There was one solitary light in the dining-room – a room all sombre oak and dull red walls as befitted a man of science – and a visiting card glistened on the table. Darbyshire read it with annoyance: 'James P Chase, *Morning Telephone*'.

'I'll have to see him,' he groaned, 'But is it possible these confounded pressmen have got hold of the story already?' Doubtless Chase was merely plunging around after sensations – the constant pestering of newspaper men was no new thing to Darbyshire with his reputation for fighting disease in bulk, the one man always sent for when there was an epidemic to be grappled with. Still, the pushing little American might have stumbled on the truth. When he came back, he had better be granted an audience, however brief. Meanwhile Darbyshire took down his telephone and churned the handle.

'Are you there? Yes, give me 30795, Kensington . . . That you, Longdale? Step round here at once, will you? Yes, I know it's hot, and I wouldn't ask you to come if it wasn't a matter of the last importance.'

He hung up his receiver, lighted a cigarette, and proceeded to con over some notes. He was roused presently by the hall bell and Dr Longdale entered. 'I suppose it's come at last?' he asked.

'Of course it has,' Darbyshire replied, 'and in a worse form than you think. Just listen to this': and he took from his pocket a news-paper clipping.

STRANGE AFFAIR AT ALDENBURGH

A day or two ago the barque *Santa Anna* came ashore at Spur, near Aldenburgh, and quickly became a total wreck. The crew of eight presumably took to their boats, for nothing has been seen of them since. How the *Santa Anna* came to be wrecked on a clear, calm night remains a mystery. From the thousands of oranges which have been picked up at Aldenburgh lately, the coastguards presume the barque to be Portuguese.

'Naturally you want to know what this has to do with us. Well, the *Santa Anna* was deliberately wrecked, and the crew for reasons of their own sank their boat. It isn't far from Aldenburgh to London: in a short time the Portuguese were in the Metropolis. Some of them set off for Cardiff, to get a ship there. On the way three are taken ill, two of them die. The local practitioner sends for the medical officer of health. The latter gets frightened and sends for me. I have just got back – with *this*.'

Darbyshire produced a phial of cloudy fluid, some of which he proceeded to lay on the glass of a powerful microscope. Longdale fairly staggered back from the eyepiece. 'Bubonic! The water reeks with the bacillus! You don't mean . . .'

'I do. This sample comes from the Thames. Those seamen, who ran their ship aground and deserted her, have been suffering from bubonic fever – and by a series of circumstances they have infected the river which gives most of London its water supply. That deadly poison is hourly drawing nearer to the metropolis into which presently it will be ladled by the million gallons. People will wash in it, drink it, Mayfair along with Whitechapel!'

'The supply must be cut off!'

'And deprive four-fifths of London of water when it is grilling like a furnace? No flushing of sewers, no watering of roads, not even a drop to drink. In two days London would be a reeking, seething hell – try and picture it!'

'There's only one alternative – that process of sterilisation of yours.'

Darbyshire smiled, and moved towards his office. The notes were there, but they seemed to have been disturbed. On the floor lay a torn sheet with shorthand cypher: thereon Darbyshire flew to the bell and rang it violently.

'Verity,' he cried when the butler appeared, 'has that Mr Chase been here again?'

'Well, he have, sir, just after Mr Longdale. So I asked him to wait, which he did, then he come out again after a bit, saying he would call again, looking very excited, sir.'

'It's clear enough,' Darbyshire turned to Longdale. 'That confounded journalist has heard all we said – and tomorrow the whole thing will be blazing in the *Telephone*. Those fellows would wreck the empire for a "scoop". But we can perhaps convince the editor that that article must not appear.' He called the butler again. 'Get me a hansom, fast as you can.'

A minute later there was a rattle of wheels outside and Darbyshire plunged hatless into the night. 'Offices of the *Telephone*. A sovereign if I'm there in twenty minutes.'

The cab plunged on headlong. The driver was going to earn that sovereign or know the reason why. He drove furiously into Trafalgar Square, a motor car crossed him recklessly, and a moment later Darbyshire was shot out onto his head. He lay there with no interest in mundane things. A crowd gathered, a doctor in evening dress appeared.

'Concussion of the brain . . . By jove, it's Darbyshire! Here, police, hurry up with the ambulance: he must be removed to Charing Cross Hospital at once.'

*   *   *

The controlling genius of the *Telephone* sat limp and bereft of coat and vest. His greeting of Chase was not over-polite. But when he saw the sheet of notes that the journalist carried, the tired look faded from his eyes. Here was the tonic his soul craved for.

'It wants pluck . . . A scare like that might ruin the Empire.'

'Take it or leave it. If you haven't got the grit, Sutton of the *Flashlight* will jump at it.'

Grady made his decision. 'Sit down right away and make two columns of it. I'll get some statistics out for you.'

Cold facts made the story seem worse, rather than better. The upper waters of the Thames were poisoned – yet nearly all London derived its water supply from those waters. Only two London water companies did not derive their water from the Thames – the New River Company and the Kent Company. Only those fortunate enough to be served by these mains would be exempt from peril – and even they would soon be in danger from their neighbours.

The further Grady read, the more he felt that if he could get this dread information into the hands of the people before it was too late, he would be playing the part of a benefactor. Desperate as the situation looked, the *Telephone* might yet save it. Professor Darbyshire had no right to hold up such a secret when he should have been taking measures to avert the threatened danger.

An hour later the presses were roaring: presently huge parcels of damp sheets were vomited into the street. London awoke, and on a hundred thousand breakfast tables the eye was arrested by scare heads:

THE POISONED THAMES

Millions of plague germs flowing down into London. Bacillus of bubonic plague in the river. New River and Kent Companies alone can supply pure water. Stupendous discovery by Professor Darbyshire. Death in your breakfast cup today. Shun it as you would poison. If you are not connected with either of the above companies, or if you have no private supply – CUT OFF YOUR WATER AT THE MAIN AT ONCE!

At eight in the morning London's pulse was calm and regular. An hour later it was writhing like some great reptile in the throes of mortal pain.

*　　*　　*

The one man who could have done most to help was lying unconscious at Charing Cross Hospital. Meanwhile Dr Longdale was the man of the hour – but he could not allay the panic that had gripped London. Under a blazing sunshine after days of heat and dust the packed East-end was suddenly deprived of every drop of water. For an hour or two no great hardship was felt, but after that every moment added to the agony. Before long the railway termini were packed with people eager to be away from the metropolis.

By midday business was at a standstill. There was not a water cart to be seen from Kensington to the Mansion House. Every cart and tank had been despatched into the New River and Kent Water area

...ell-dressed business men could ... seen proceeding in cabs to ... favoured area with buckets ...d water cars.

61

to convey a supply as speedily as possible to the congested districts East and South-east of the Thames. By lunchtime the City presented a strange spectacle. Well-dressed business men could be seen proceeding in cabs with buckets and water cans with the object of taking a supply forthwith. Cabmen were commanding their own prices.

Mineral waters went up 200% in price: by midday the supply had ceased – men of means with an eye to the future had bought up the whole stock. The streets were crowded with people anxiously awaiting developments. They were rewarded a little after two o'clock when a boy came yelling down the Strand with a flapping of papers on his shoulder: 'The plague broken out! Two cases of bubonic fever at Limehouse! Speshull!'

Perhaps if the readers had known these two cases were renegades from the *Santa Anna,* the panic might have been allayed. But nobody knew. Though no fever could have broken out so soon, it was assumed that the two poor fellows had drunk of the polluted flood and paid the penalty. It might be the turn of any of them next. There were those who shrugged their shoulders stolidly, others that crept into bars and restaurants and asked furtively for brandy.

By this time everything that could be done was being done. The artesian wells of East and South London were being tapped. Private houses which possessed pumps were besieged. Main line trains made way for trains of tanks bringing water to the city. But the problem of distribution remained – how could the little water available be distributed fairly among six million people over an area of some thirty square miles?

Night came, but brought no end to the stream of people coming and going between Trafalgar Square and such other open supplies as were available. Morning brought the promise of another sweltering day. Smartly dressed men were to be seen with grimy chins and features frankly dirty. The dust in the unwatered streets became intolerable. Tempers were strained. Small riots broke out here and there, some people were robbed of their precious fluid as they carried it home. Democratic agitators took advantage of the situation, a mob stormed the Houses of Parliament singing the Marseillaise in strident tones. Looters ravaged the markets, went off with baskets of apples and oranges. Mysteriously, as the sign that called up the Indian Mutiny, the signal went round to raid the public houses and hotels. Men stood in the Strand outside famous restaurants with bottles of strange liquids in their hands, the necks of which they knocked off without ceremony to reach the precious fluid within.

What might have happened when these last scant resources gave out will fortunately never be known. For suddenly, beneath the hubbub of the streets, the clamour and shrieks of the rioters, a strange unbelievable sound was heard. The shouting died away – and the people of London heard it now with no mistaking: the sound of water! The water supply had been restored!

The turnocks in the **Strand** were busy flushing the gutters with standpipes, a row of fire engines were proceeding to wash the streets down from the mains. The whole thing was so sudden and unexpected that it seemed like a dream.

And what was even less expected – what people only learnt when they read their papers that evening – was that the city's water supply was safe to drink all these days. For what Dr Darbyshire had no time to tell his colleague, in his hurry to get to the *Telephone* offices, was that as soon as he realised the pollution of the water at Ashchurch, he had applied his sterilising process on the spot. A few miles further down the river, the water gave the result of perfect purity.

But for the accident in Trafalgar Square, there would have been no untoward consequences: but Dr Longdale, having seen the bacillus-infested water, and not knowing of the sterilisation, had no alternative but to cut off the water supply forthwith.

London that night was in a frenzy of elation. Men shook one another by the hand, hats were cast into the air and forgotten: people stood under the beating drip of the fire-engines' sluicing until they were soaked to the skin: well-dressed men laved themselves in the clear running gutters. London was saved from disaster, and Dr Darbyshire was the hero of the hour.

'All the same, it was a near thing, Longdale. Some day perhaps this country will realise what a debt it owes to its men of science – and perhaps learn to foster them a little more. For nothing but science could, these past days, have prevented a calamity that would have multiplied ten-fold the horrors of the Great Plague, and destroyed not thousands, but tens of thousands.'

e mob filled the chamber, ling and shouting. It was in n that the Speaker tried to ke his voice heard above the

63

LONDON'S DANGER

by CUTCLIFFE HYNE

HE first-class carriage we were in was heated by steam, we had each abundance of coats and rugs, our feet were on a fresh foot-warmer; but the draught of the hurricane crept in by a score of chinks, and I noted that Gerard's moustache glistened with icicles.

'Nice weather this for getting married in!' I remarked. 'If we'd had warning of this blizzard I should either have shirked being your best man, or suggested having the affair postponed.'

'If tomorrow's like this, the wedding can't take place. It would be brutal to drag any woman out into such a nipping cold.'

At Grantham we saw men filling the engine with buckets from a well outside the station, because the ordinary water supply was frozen solid; the conductor, purple-cheeked and blowing his fingers, told us that both driver and stoker were half-perished with exposure, that it was doubtful whether one of them would recover, but that substitutes were being sought to take us on to London. He told us, too, that news had been brought down of a colossal fire in West London, but could add no details.

Eventually the train began to move again, and slid out of Grantham into the open country. The south-westerly hurricane beat upon it till the flanges of the lee wheels grated upon the rails with a roar of sound; in some of the heavier squalls I thought we should be upset. But with dogged slowness we crawled on, and drew up under the shelter of Kings Cross station.

It was four o'clock, and we were three hours late. There was a bellow of life from the departure side of the station, but where we were the place seemed deserted. Not a porter to be seen, and only one hansom on the rank. We got into that lonely cab, and told the muffled driver to take us to Kensington. As the glass door was clattering down, a boy thrust a paper at us.

'Evening paper, sir? There's half Chelsea on fire.'

'Give him a penny, Methuen,' Gerard said.

'Five bob or nothing, sir. I've only two papers left, and there's ten firemen killed. They say half London will be burnt.'

I fumbled out two half-crowns, and the cab drove off. I scanned the headlines: DISASTROUS FIRE. FANNED BY THE FURIOUS GALE. ALL HYDRANTS FROZEN. EVERY DROP OF WATER IN LONDON SOLID ICE. NOTHING TO CHECK THE FLAMES. METROPOLIS IN TERRIBLE DANGER. SUICIDE OF THE CHIEF OF THE FIRE BRIGADE. And in the light of the strange lurid glare which lit the sky, I read the smaller print:

The fire in Hammersmith has assumed gigantic proportions. The united fire brigades of London are helpless to cope with it. The unprecedented severity of the frost, and the fury of the hurricane which is now upon us, have made all precautions futile. It is with water alone that our fire-extinguishing services have been armed: and now in this moment of desperate need even a trickle of water is denied them.

Hammersmith is now a burnt-out rubbish heap. West Kensington is a furnace. In South Kensington and Chelsea there is panic. So far as human eye can see, nothing but a change of wind or an act of God can save the greatest city ever built by man from being in the next few hours changed to twisted, smoking ruins.

Gerard thrust up the hatch. 'A fiver if you keep your horse at a gallop,' he shouted. 'My God, Methuen, what an awful thing this is!'

'The newspaper has made the worst of it for the sake of the sensation. London isn't built of wood: it is impossible for the whole of it to burn.'

'I'm thinking of Queen's Gate, and my little girl there. She expected me three hours ago.'

The cab stopped with a jar against the kerb. I scraped the frost from the window and peered out. We were in Piccadilly – and the street was one solid block of every imaginable kind of vehicle, bearing salvage and fugitives eastwards. With infinite trouble our cabman wormed his way across the struggling mass, but Gerard's impatience grew too great. He sprang from the cab, gave the man a ten-pound note with orders to follow as best he could, and started off through the hurrying crowds on foot.

Then for the first time we began fully to realise the fright which had bitten into five millions of people. The most orderly city on earth had turned into a seething nest of anarchy. And as we went on, with the gale beating in our faces, we ourselves became smitten with the prevailing spirit, jostling and thrusting at everyone who came in our way. Three times I saw bodies lying motionless in my path, and the passers-by cursed as they stumbled against them. but no one stopped to help.

And once I saw a woman of elegant dress, who was driving a landau filled with trunks and boxes, drop the reins when a heavy dray cut off one of her wheels, and pull out a pistol and kill herself before a thousand lookers-on. But no one gave her more than a cursory glance. Each one looked ahead on his own path, and hurried away about his business.

The air grew warmer as we pressed on westwards. There was no glimpse of flame apparent yet, but fat black rolls of smoke could be seen overhead, with an underlining of yellow reflected from the distant blaze. And everywhere hung icicles, and the lines of the bursted water-mains glistened in the roadways. There was the taint of burning in every breath we drew, and from the inky sky above fell a constant patter of charred embers. As we drew on, these embers grew bright, and by the time we were through Brompton (and seven had clanged from some clock in the neighbourhood) live sparks were falling on the seething mobs and the air was sour with the smell of singeing cloth.

Abreast of the South Kensington Museum, the flames were glowing yellow against the black clouds of smoke: the thunder of the blaze and the crash of falling masonry came in a dim roar above the booming and swishing of the gale. The great warren of dwelling-houses to westward of us yielded up its thousand emigrants every minute. The fugitives had started out of home hugging their dearest possessions: but the sacking of their city thrust terror into their hearts and taught them that naked life is dearer than all else the world contains. So the streets were paved with loads of rarities which lay in the roadways as though they had been so much coal.

The fire was advancing whole streets by the hour. The volcano shower fell more thickly as we moved westward, while the crowd thinned nearer the heart of the blaze. When we turned up Queen's

Gate the street, though half filled by furniture and debris, was almost deserted by human beings. Gerard was nearly beside himself with foreboding when we reached the house. He dashed up the steps – and the girl he thought to make his bride stood waiting for him in the doorway.

'Oh, my love,' I heard her say as she leant on his shoulder. 'I am here alone. They have all gone. But you said you would come for me: and I knew you would if you were alive; and if you were not, I did not wish to live either.'

But meanwhile the heat was growing upon us, and whilst I stood and watched, I saw flames beginning to spout from the upper windows of a house near the Cromwell Road. 'Look, we must go. This house will be burning in another ten minutes.' At the word Miss Vivian picked up a jewel-case and came with Gerard down the steps. We began walking northwards, and as we were passing Queen's Gate Terrace a man joined us whom I knew. His name is an old and honoured one, but I omit it here for the sake of others who have borne the title.

'Oh, I am beggared!' he cried. 'What is that you have? Jewels?' He snatched the morocco box from Miss Vivian's hands. 'I must have something, I refuse to starve!' and he ran off howling.
A van stood in the roadway, with horses trembling and snorting. 'The law is dead,' I said, 'Every man takes what he wants now. Jump in.'

The horses sprang away at a gallop. At the end of the street was a tangled block of furniture, into which a hansom cab had crashed: the horse had broken a leg and lay moving feebly. But it was no time for hesitation. I charged my team at the barrier, and with a crash and a bang and a rattle we were over. I headed for the Marble Arch, intending to get to one of the railway stations where we could run away north out of this horrible city of fire and terror. But past Hyde Park Corner I could get the van no farther. The roadways were piled up to the doors of the houses on either side with a mass of vehicles, and alive with madly plunging horses. Never was known such a scene since the world began. And there they were doomed to wait, in that inextricable tangle, till the flames swept up and ground them into smoke.

We deserted our van and hand-in-hand we skirted that awful block. We rounded Buckingham Palace only to find Victoria Street impassable. Of a sudden the air was split by a terrific roar: another followed: and another. The pavement beneath us shook, and the tall houses on either side shed dust. The gale for a moment stopped: then hit us with a fresh blast which there was no standing against: and then a tornado of dust and fragments swept down so thick that we could scarcely catch a breath. They were blowing up a line of houses along the forefront of the fire, in the desperate hope that the flames would not leap the gap.

By a sort of dull instinct I was heading for the east. For hours that

We made our way across to the southern shore.

seemed like years I struggled on like a man in a dream, with one hand dragging at Miss Vivian and the other wrestling with the people who thronged us. The crowd was a frightened sheep-pack, scattering before the wolves of flame, each in his blind terror ready to trample down his neighbour. At Charing Cross Station the press was so great that the lines were blocked with writhing humanity, and no train could get in across the bridge. Then a thought occurred to me: The river was frozen, we could make passage across the ice.

With the breath of the advancing flames hot upon our faces we went down the steps by Cleopatra's Needle, and got on the frozen surface without so much as a shoe wet. Along with thousands of others on that ice, we made our way across to the southern bank. The buildings there had escaped the conflagration, and men stood on the silhouetted roofs to keep flying embers from finding a lodgement.

But of the other side, which we had left, who could put in mere words the grandeur and awfulness of the sight! It seemed as though the great city had been first gripped by a polar winter, and was now being snatched back by the powers of hell. We watched on as the blaze drove eastwards, and saw it bite the end of the Strand, and then from the great shelter of Charing Cross Station there came a stream of shrieks which made us shudder. That, too, had been ravished by the flames, and of the thousands within it, all who could not escape were being baked alive, or crushed by the falling roof.

But meanwhile the freezing gale sweeping down the river was nipping us with a more physical chill, and Miss Vivian was almost fainting with the exposure. We made our way to the Waterloo Road, crammed with fugitives, but more orderly here where the danger was not so imminent. We found a cab, and by offering enough gold succeeded in being driven to Dulwich, where Gerard had friends.

That is the last I saw of the burning of London, though we saw the glare of it in the sky for five awful days, while it gutted the whole of the City and almost all North London, turned into crumbling ruins the Bank of England and the Tower, blasted out of existence the slums of Wapping and the Mile End Road, burnt the shipping and the warehouses, the shops and the offices – and by one means or another caused the death of five hundred thousand of the population.

Yes; half a million human beings perished in that awful tornado of flame, or died of the subsequent exposure and want: three hundred thousand more were changed from householders into homeless outcasts: but figures will give no idea of the vast amount of property that was blotted out of existence. Not only was solid, visible wealth wafted away in smoke, but the national credit was blasted and the bourses of the outside world smitten to their foundations. Civilisation has received no such shock since Atlantis sank beneath the ocean waves. In the hour of our pride we boasted that no nation on earth could lay us low. But the elements were set to war against our might, and they have humbled the British Empire even unto the ground.

4 Around the world in any number of ways

Accounts of travels above and beneath the earth's surface, all written before the Wright Brothers' success

From Pole to Pole *(George Griffith, 1903)*

The Fate of the Firefly *(The Rev. J. M. Bacon F.R.A.S. 1901)*

The Abduction of Alexandra Seine *(Fred C. Smale, 1900)*

In 1877 a patent for an air cushion vehicle was taken out by John Isaac Thornycroft, the marine engineer. To test his ideas, he adapted the design of one of his own vessels, the torpedo-boat 'Lightning'. If only suitable materials had been available, his proposition would have been an entirely practicable one — and the hovercraft of which we in the 1970s are so proud would have been anticipated by close on a century.

It doesn't do to underestimate the Victorians. It was lack of materials, not lack of imagination, which prevented them from making strides as great as those we have made in our own day. Where materials allowed, progress was rapid. When the muddy rutted track which passed for a road in 1837 had been replaced by a smooth macadamised roadway, the vehicles which used the road could be improved in turn. When steam power was made practicable, it was rapidly exploited. So were electricity, and hydraulics, and pneumatic power, and eventually the internal combustion engine.

The Victorians were magnificently ingenious, too, when one-off problems had to be solved — constructing steamer-trains for the broad Indian waterways, improvising amphibious vessels for African explorers, using balloons for meteorological research, or creating a special vessel to float Cleopatra's Needle from Egypt to England.

And they were eager to venture further — they had dreams of developing almost every known method of locomotion. On land they invented ice-cars and sand-cars: gyrocars and monorails: electric trams and carriages:

BY BALLOON TO THE POLE

Many explorers believed that balloons offered the best chance of reaching the elusive Pole, and Commander Cheyne's 1897 plan was only one of many. But when, later the same year, the Swedish aeronaut Andrée did actually set off, he vanished and no trace of him or his balloons was found for more than thirty years.

adaptations without number of skating and cycling. On sea, steamers with twin hulls plied the English Channel from Dover to Calais: a vessel named the Connector, with a jointed hull which enabled it to be divided into three separate vessels, completed successful trial trips: there were spectactular schemes to sail across the Atlantic in gondolas drawn by kites. And in the air, besides all the many attempts to produce a navigable flying-machine which would not be a slave to the winds, there were plans to use the devices they already possessed — balloons — to carry man to the North Pole, plans which ended in the ill-fated but wonderfully courageous expedition of Major Andrée.

Truly, if the old lady who declared that if the Almighty had meant man to fly he would have given us wings ever existed, she was not a typical representative of Victoria's generation!

FROM POLE TO POLE

by GEORGE GRIFFITH

ELL, Professor, what is it? Something pretty important, I suppose, from the wording of your note. Have you solved the problem of aerial navigation, or got a glimpse into the fourth dimension?'

'Not any of those as yet, my friend, but something that may be quite as wonderful.'

'Well, if it is something really extraordinary and at the same time practicable, I'm there as far as the financial part goes. As regards the scientific end of the business, if you say "Yes" it is "Yes".'

Mr Arthur Princeps had good reasons for thus 'going blind' on a project of which he knew nothing save that it probably meant a scientific gamble to the tune of several thousand pounds. Professor Haffkin was a man rich in ideas but comparatively poor in money: Arthur had both ideas and money, and as a result of this conjunction the man of science had made thousands out of his inventions, while the scientific man of business had made tens of thousands by exploiting them.

Next day there was a strong, steady breeze blowing directly from the northward. The great kites were sent up, six in all, and along the fine piano-wire cables which held them, the lighter portions of the stores were sent on carriers driven by smaller kites. Princeps and Brenda had gone up first in the carrier-slings. The Professor remained on the beach with the bluejackets who were giving a helping hand in the strangest job that even British sailors had ever helped to put through. Their remarks formed a commentary as original as it was terse: it had, however, the disadvantage of being mostly unprintable.

Some hours later, after shaking hands all round, the Professor took his seat in the sling of the last kite and went soaring up over the summit of the ice-wall. A pull on the tilting-line brought the great kite slowly to the ground. As the cable slackened, it was released from its moorings on the beach. A little engine, driven by liquid air, hauled it up on a drum – cutting the last link between them and the rest of the world.

The three members of the Pole to Pole Expedition bivouacked that night under a snow-knoll: after a good sleep they set to work on the preparations for the last stage but one of their voyage. There were four sledges. One formed the baggage-wagon; it carried the gas-cylinders, the greater part of the provisions, and the vehicle which was to carry the three adventurers through the centre of the Earth. It was packed in sections, to be put together when the edge of the great hole was reached.

The sledge could be driven by two means. As long as the north-to-south wind held good, it was dragged over the ice by the kites. It was also furnished with a liquid-air engine which actuated four big spiked wheels, which would grip the frozen snow and drive the sledge runners at 20 mph, when the wind was light or non-existent. The other three kites were smaller but similar in construction. One carried provisions; another was loaded with the tents and cooking apparatus; the third carried the three passengers.

They travelled for six uneventful days, spinning softly over the undulating fields of snow-covered ice with scarcely a jog or a jar – as Brenda said, it was more like a 1200-mile switchback than a polar expedition. Overhead were the great box-kites, high in the air, dull white against the dim blue sky, dragging them so swiftly towards the Unknown – and perhaps the Impossible.

On the seventh morning the kites were lowered, with the exception of one which drew the big sledge. They were now within a hundred miles of the Pole, and could expect any moment to reach the edge of the tunnel whose diameter could be anything from 50 to 100 miles across. So the liquid-air engines were set to work, and the sledges moved forward at a cautious eight miles per hour.

A little before lunch-time the ground began to slope suddenly away to the south to such an extent that the last kite was hauled in, and the spiked wheels had to be used to check the increasing speed of the sledges. After a descent of about an hour, they could see a vast curved ridge of snow stretching to right and left behind them, shutting out the almost level rays of the pale sun. Taking to their snowshoes, they moved cautiously forward to investigate: after about a mile and a half they came to the edge of what appeared to be an ice-cliff.

'I wonder if it really *is* the Tunnel?' said Brenda, taking a step forward.

'Whatever it is, it's too deep for you to fall into with any comfort,' said her husband, dragging her back almost roughly. Almost at the same moment a mass of ice and snow on which they had been standing a few moments before, broke away and disappeared into the void. They listened with all their ears, but no sound came back: the huge block had vanished in silence into nothingness, into a void which had apparently no bottom; for even if it had fallen a thousand feet, an echo would have come back to them up the wall.

'But uncle, if this is the Tunnel, and that block of ice has gone on before us, won't it stop and come back when it gets near the North Pole? Suppose we were to meet it?'

'There is no fear of a collision. You see, there is atmosphere in the tunnel, and long before it reaches the centre, friction will have melted the ice and dissipated the water into vapour.'

Now it was time to set to work on the preparations for the last stage of the journey. The sledges dissolved into their component parts, and these came together again in the form of a big, conical, drum-like structure, with walls of thick papier mache. It had four long plate-glass windows in the sides and a large round one top and bottom. It was 10 feet in diameter and 15 feet in height. The interior was plainly but snugly fitted up as a sitting-room by day and, by means of a movable partition, a couple of sleeping-berths by night. Food and water were stowed in cupboards and tanks beneath the seats, and the gas-cylinders, rockets etc. were packed under the flooring. The liquid-air engines and the driving apparatus of the sledges were strongly secured to the lower end with chains which, in case of emergency, could be easily released by slip-hooks operated from inside. There were also 200 pounds of shot-ballast. Attached to the upper part were four balloons, capable of lifting the projectile with its whole load on board. These were connected by tubes with the interior and thus, by means of pumps, the gas from the cylinders could either be driven up into them or drawn down and re-stored. In the centre of the roof was another cable, longer than those which held the balloons, and to this was attached a large parachute which could be opened or shut at will from inside.

*   *   *

The balloons were inflated until the *Brenda* – as the strange vehicle had been named by a majority of two to one – began to pull at the ropes. Then, with a last look round the inhospitable land they were leaving – perchance never to see land of any sort again – they went in through the curved sliding door. Princeps started the engine: the balloons began to fill out: and three of the ropes were cast off as the *Brenda* began to rock and swing.

'One more,' said Princeps, giving his wife the knife. She gave her land hand to her husband, knelt down on the threshold of the door, and made a sideward slash at the slender rope. The strands ripped and parted, the *Brenda* rocked, the ice-cliffs slipped away from under them, the vast, unfathomed and fathomless gulf spread out beneath them, and the voyage, either from Pole to Pole or from Time to Eternity, had begun.

The Professor allowed the *Brenda* to drift for two and a half hours at a carefully calculated wind-speed of 20 mph. Then he said 'You can deflate the balloons now. We must be near the centre.' He turned to cast loose the fine wire cables which held the ribs of the parachute. The gas from the balloons hissed back into the cylinders. The envelopes were hauled in and stowed away. Through the top window Brenda saw the full disc of the moon growing smaller and smaller, and she knew they had begun their fall of 41,708,711 feet.

Taking this as 7000 miles in round numbers, the Professor, reckoning on an average speed of 50 to 60 mph, expected to make the passage in about six days. As events proved, they made it in a good deal less. For the first 36 hours everything went with perfect smoothness. The wind-gauges showed a speed of 51 mph: the *Brenda* continued her fall with perfect steadiness.

'I am going to ask you to believe something,' the Professor said on this occasion, 'which I dare say you will think impossible. It's a journey through the centre of the earth.'

'*Through* the centre? But the centre of the earth is a solid body, harder and denser than anything we know on the surface.'

By way of answer, the Professor got up from his chair and went to a cupboard. He took out a glass vessel about 6 inches in diameter and 12 in height, and placed it on a table.

The vessel was filled with a fluid which looked like water. Exactly halfway down was a spherical globule of a brownish-yellow colour, about an inch in diameter. As the Professor set the glass down the globule oscillated a little, then came to rest. Then he took a long thin steel needle with a little disc of thin white metal fixed about 3 inches from the end. He lowered it into the fluid and passed it through the middle of the globule, which broke as the disc passed into it, then re-shaped itself again in perfectly spherical form about it.

'This is a globule of coloured oil. It floats in a mixture of alcohol and water which is of exactly the same specific gravity as its own. It thus represents as nearly as possible the earth in its former molten condition, floating in space. The earth had then, as now, a rotary action on its own axis. This needle represents that axis. I give it a rotary motion, and you will see what happened to our planet millions of years ago.'

As he said this he began to twirl the needle swiftly but very steadily. The globule flattened and spread out laterally until it became a ring. Then the twirling slowed down. The ring became a globule again, but flattened at either pole, and there was a clearly defined circular hole through it from pole to pole. The Professor deftly withdrew the needle and disc through the opening, and the globule continued to revolve round the hole through its centre.

'There is the earth as I believe it to be today. The exterior crust has cooled. Inside it is a semi-fluid sphere; inside that again, possibly, the rigid body, the core of the earth. But I don't believe that hole has been filled. Granted that the pull of gravitation is towards the centre, still, if there is a void from Pole to Pole, as I hold there must be as a natural consequence of the centrifugal force generated by the earth's revolution, the mass of the earth would pull equally in all directions away from that void.'

'I think I see,' said Princeps. 'Granted a passage like that from

Pole to Pole – call it a tunnel – a body falling into it at one end would be drawn towards the centre. It would pass it at a tremendous velocity and be carried towards the other end; but as the attraction of the mass of the earth would be equal on all sides of it, it would take a perfectly direct course – I mean, it wouldn't smash itself against the sides of the tunnel. The only difficulty I see is that, suppose the body were dropped into the tunnel at the North Pole, it wouldn't quite reach the South Pole. It would stop and turn back, and so it would oscillate like a pendulum with an ever-decreasing swing until it came to rest in the centre of the earth.'

'Exactly,' said the Professor, 'but means could be taken to propel the projectile beyond the attraction from the centre, at the moment when the momentum of the body was being counteracted by the return pull towards the centre.'

'Perfectly feasible,' Princeps agreed, 'provided there were reasonable beings in the said projectile. Well, I think I understand you now. Which Pole do you propose to start from?'

'The North Pole, though still undiscovered, is getting a little bit hackneyed. I propose that we shall start from the South Pole . . . Of course you realise that you cannot hope for any monetary return, and it is also quite possible that we may both lose our lives?'

'People who stick at small things never do great ones,' was Princeps' reply.

*   *   *

Nearly two months after this conversation, something else happened. The Professor's niece came back from Heidelberg with her degree of Doctor of Philosophy. Certain former experiences had led Princeps to the opinion that she liked him exceedingly for himself, and disliked him almost as much for his money – a fact which made the possession of millions seem very unprofitable in his eyes.

Brenda Haffkin happened to get back to London the day after everything had been arranged for the most amazing and seemingly impossible expedition that human beings had ever attempted. The Royal Geographical Society of London was sending out a couple of vessels to the frozen land of Antarctica. A splendid donation to the expedition's funds had procured a passage in one of them for the adventurers and about ten tons of baggage, the ultimate use of which was little dreamt of by any other member of the expedition.

The secret was broken to Brenda about a week before the start of the expedition. Whatever she thought of the project, she betrayed no sign of belief or disbelief; but when the Professor had finished his explanation, she turned to Princeps. 'And are you really going on this expedition, risking probable starvation and more than probable destruction, let alone spending a great deal of money?'

'Why not? If we find there really is a tunnel through the earth, and take a series of electro-cinematograph photographs of the crust and core of the earth, we shall have done something that no one else

She had looked over the great Ice Wall of the South.

has thought about. I don't see how a man in my position could spend his money and risk his life much better.'

There was a little silence, then Brenda said 'I should like to come too.'

'You could only do that on one condition. And that is, that you say "Yes" to a question you said "No" to nine months ago.'

'If you'll let me come with you, I will . . . You see, I didn't think you were in earnest about these things before. But now I see you are, and that makes you very different, you know . . .' She was in his arms by this time, and the discussion speedily reached a satisfactory, if partially inarticulate, conclusion.

*　　　*　　　*

The quiet wedding by special licence, and the voyage from Southampton to Victoria Land, were very much like other weddings and other voyages: but when the ships anchored under the smoke-shadow of Mount Terror and the mysterious cases were opened, the officers and crew began to have grave doubts as to the sanity of their passengers. There were little cylinders of a curiously light metal, with screw-taps on either end of them – about two thousand of them. There were also queer 'fitments', which, when they were landed, somehow erected themselves into sledges with cog-wheels alongside them. There were also little balloons, filled out of the taps of the cylinders, which went up attached to big box-kites. When the wind was sufficiently strong, and blowing in the right direction towards the Southern Pole, a combination of these kites took up Professor Haffkin and then Mr Princeps and finally, after many protestations, Mrs Princeps. She, happening to get to the highest elevation, came down and reported that she had seen what no other Northern-borne human being had ever seen.

She had looked over the great Ice Wall of the South, and from the summit of it she had seen nothing but an illimitable plain of snow-prairies, here and there broken up by a few ice-mountains, stretching away beyond the limit of vision to the South. There was nothing to prevent their starting on the 1200 mile journey to the Pole.

Suddenly, just as they were about to say 'Good night' for the second time, they heard a sharp snapping and rending sound break through the smooth swish of the air. The next instant their vehicle rocked violently from side to side, and the indicators of the gauges began to fly round into invisibility.

'It can only be one thing,' said the Professor. 'Some of the stays have given way, and the parachute has split or broken up. God forgive me, why did I not think of it before – the increasing pull of gravitation as we get nearer to the centre. I calculated for a uniform pull only. They must have been bearing a tremendous strain before they parted.'

The vehicle had become steady again, but the rush of wind past the outside wall deepened to a roar, then rose to a shrill scream. Long moments of sheer speechless terror passed. The air grew hot, stifling. Even the uninflammable walls began to crinkle and crack under the fearful heat developed by the friction. Brenda gasped for breath, then fell fainting on the floor. Mechanically, her husband stooped to lift her up. To his amazement, the effort he made nearly threw her unconscious form to the top of the conical roof. She floated in mid-air for a moment, then sank gently back into their arms.

'The Centre of the Earth!' gasped the Professor. 'The point of equal attraction! If we can breathe for the next hour, we have a chance!' They had passed the centre of the earth at an enormous but unknown velocity: their momentum would certainly carry them far towards the northern end of the Axial Tunnel. Hours passed, and then at last the rush of wind began to slacken. The wind gauge registered a little over 200 mph.

'Our only chance,' said the Professor, looking up from his calculations, 'is to watch that indicator till the speed drops to, say, ten miles an hour. Then we inflate our balloons to the utmost, cut loose the engines and other gear, and trust to the gas to pull us out.'

Hour by hour the speed dropped. Somewhere, an unknown number of miles above them, were the solitudes of the Northern Pole. Below was the awful gulf through which they had already passed, but into which they would once more fall if the balloons failed to do their job. The Professor busied himself with calculations relating to the amount of gas at their disposal, its lifting power, and the weights involved. His results he kept to himself: he had the best of reasons for doing so.

The hours went by. The speed dropped steadily – 100 mph had become 50, 50 became 40, then 30, 20 and 10. 'You can get your balloons out now, Arthur. It's a good thing we housed them in time, or they would have been torn to ribbons.'

Within an hour the four balloons were cast loose through their portholes in the roof of the car. Meanwhile the upward speed of the *Brenda* had dropped from ten to seven miles. The balloons began to fill: for a few moments the indicator stopped still – then rose to seven, eight, nine. But at ten the little steel hand, which to them was veritably the Hand of Fate, began to creep slowly backwards again.

None of them spoke. They all knew what it meant. The upward pull of the balloons was not counteracting the downward pull from the centre of the earth. In a few hours more they would come to a standstill: then, when the two forces balanced, they would hang motionless in that awful gulf of everlasting night until the gas gave out, and then the backward plunge to perdition would begin.

'I think we may let the engines go now, Arthur,' said the Professor. 'It's quite evident that we're overweighted.' He said this in a whisper because Brenda, utterly worn out, had gone to lie down behind the partition.

The hooks were slipped, and the hand on the dial began to move again. But the speed rose only to 15 mph: the attractive force was evidently being exerted from the sides of the tunnel as well as from the centre of the earth. The Professor looked at the dial and said to Princeps: 'We're doing nicely now. I think you'd better go and lie down while I stand watch. I hope we shall be through our difficulties by the morning.'

He got his papers out again and once more went through the maze of figures and formulae. Then, when the sound of deep breathing told him that Princeps was asleep, he opened the trap-door to count the unexhausted cylinders of gas. 'Barely enough to get them home, even with the best of luck: but still enough to prove that it is possible to make a journey from Pole to Pole. At least that will be done and proved – and Karl Haffkin will live for ever.'

There was the look of martyrdom in his eyes as he looked for the last time at the dial. Then he unscrewed the circular window from the bottom of the car, lowered himself through it, hung for a moment to the edge with his hands, and let go.

*   *   *

When Princeps and Brenda woke they were astonished to find the windows of the car glowing with a strange, brilliant light – the light of the Northern Aurora. Princeps jumped to his feet: 'Hurrah, Professor! We've got there!'

He hung for a moment to the edge with his hands, and let go.

But there was no Professor, and only the open trap-door and the window hanging on its hinges below told how a priceless life had been heroically sacrificed. Without Karl Haffkin's martyrdom, the great experiment must have failed, and three lives would have been lost instead of one. So he chose to die the lesser death so that he himself might live for ever on the roll of honour emblazoned with the names of the noblest of all martyrs – those who have given their lives to prove that Truth is true.

THE FATE OF THE FIREFLY.

by the REV. J. M. BACON F.R.A.S.

T is now no breach of confidence if I make known to the world – for the first time – the fate of the only contrivance that has ever fairly deserved the name of a flying-machine. I have no word to say here about machines as fly only on paper, or that buzz about a lecture-room and weigh only a few ounces: or again about those mammoth machines which have met only with disaster; but those who are interested in the circumstances of an aerial voyage unparalleled in history will find the following narrative not without interest.

At the date of which I write I was passing an autumn holiday in Yorkshire with my niece and ward, Mabel. One morning she asked, with an assumption of carelessness, 'Shall we walk to the Cove after lunch? Mr Broughton will be there at four, and he promises to show us his workshop.'

It was at Broughton's recommendation that we were visiting this part of the country. A distinguished member of the Institution of Engineers, he had a workshop in the vicinity of which we had vaguely heard many things, but which we had not hitherto been privileged to visit. When we arrived there that afternoon, we found it littered with such lumber as you may find outside a smith's or wheelwright's shop. There were a lathe, a bench, a circular saw, and long racks of tools. All this one understood, but under a huge sky-light and occupying all the centre space there stood a weird-looking contrivance that was wholly unintelligible. It might have been the skeleton of some antediluvian monster bird or flying fish. There were huge lateral wings, in texture like a bat's, there was a pointed beak and a neck whose vertebrae were jointed pully blocks, but the body was too complex for comprehension, though it clearly contained an engine of some sort, with a tank which also did duty as a table.

The machine was proudly sailing over the trees and making fast out towards the sea.

'It's the work of five years,' the proud inventor told us. 'See here, I have been putting it in working order to show you. Hold your hats on!'

He laid his hand on the creature's shoulder and depressed a lever, and then I understood the smell of mineral oil that pervaded the place. There was a click, a whirr and a rattle, as with a mighty blast a maze of fans broke into rapid motion bewilderingly. It was beautiful, it was tremendous, and one suddenly felt as if in some wonderful presence.

With a pretty little scream Mabel said it was better than the sea breeze, and begged to know what in the world it all was meant for.

'This is the Firefly. It is a flying-machine, and I promise you it won't be long now before it can fly. It has abundant power, but the angle of the aero-planes has scarcely yet the proper relation to the position of the centre of gravity. This is simply a matter of trial and it is already nearly right. But let us have some tea.'

With this he unpacked a basket and spread the contents on the table already mentioned. He requested Mabel to take the seat in the machine – 'It is the seat of honour, and I want you to try how beautifully the thing balances. Get out, Carlo,' he ordered the St Bernard hound who had jumped in after Mabel. But the girl begged that the dog might remain, and the next moment a terrible thing happened.

Broughton moved away to shift some struts and so allow the machine to poise itself, and at that moment the heavy dog must have sat back against one of the levers. There was a whirr and rattle as before, only ten times more furious, and then Mabel uttered a cry of terror: 'Oh Charley, what is it doing?'

Had he been nearer he might have done something. Had I known what to do, I should certainly have done it: but the angry fans beat me off, and the next moment the machine lifted itself clear out through the open skylight, and so flew away.

Frantically we rushed outside, but only in time to see the machine proudly sailing over the trees and making fast out towards the sea in the twilight. My poor niece looking back cried out in agony 'What am I to do?' In reply my companion, with greater promptitude than I could have summoned at such a moment, shouted 'Leave it quite alone and don't fear. We will follow.'

We did follow, wildly, as far as we could: but it was soon out over the sea, travelling as fast as a train, so that in two or three minutes it was lost in the gathering darkness.

'I believe she is safe,' Broughton exclaimed. 'Somehow that blessed machine has got its balance at last and flies steady as a bird. With this wind they will be across the sea before morning. The only thing that troubles me is that your niece will not know how to stop or alight. Oh, if only I were there!'

There was only one thing for it – and so, an hour after midnight, we were on the night boat to Hamburg, pacing the deck restlessly. 'If my poor niece escapes, she may possibly wire before we reach Hamburg, in which case the telegram will be forwarded and we shall find it on our arrival. If this is not so, we may prosecute what inquiries we can.'

The predicament, awful as it was, certainly appeared somewhat less appalling as we considered it more calmly. By happy chance there were provisions for the poor voyager ready to hand. There was nothing to fear on the score of cold, for aerial travellers at night find the upper air much warmer than that below, moreover the furnace stove was a source of warmth. I had perfect confidence in my niece's courage, and by morning light it was our hope that she would be over the land.

A sickening dread overtook us, though, when we reached our destination and found no message awaiting us. Had the young mechanician's calculations been ill-founded? We made enquiries of vessels arriving in the town as to whether any unusual object had been seen in sea or sky or land, but heard nothing until the fourth day, when my eye caught the following in a Danish paper: 'Considerable curiosity was excited yesterday morning in the little village of D— by the appearance of a strange dog of the St Bernard breed, bearing round his neck, secured by a lady's handkerchief, a message in English as of distress, hastily written. Inquiries in the neighbourhood have so far failed to disclose the owner of the strange visitor'.

Within an hour we were in pursuit of this clue. Travelling by day and night we reached our destination the following evening – to be greeted by Broughton's dog, eloquently beseeching his master's sympathy in a strange land. But we were fated to have our hopes shaken by the message of which the faithful animal had been the bearer: 'Twice touched ground. Cannot get out. Help!'

It was easy to grasp that unless the engine of the machine were first stopped, its occupant would find it impossible to alight on account of the revolving fans. But Broughton's view was more penetrating. 'I see it all now. I had forgotten about the dog. I had been reckoning that as the machine grew lighter with consumption of oil it would gradually ascend, whereas on the contrary it has slightly descended. Carlo, sitting in the bow, would make the airship pitch forward somewhat. The dog altered the balance from the first, and had he remained in the machine it must presently have run itself to ground. But either the dog of its own accord jumped out, or more probably was induced to do so.'

'But what would happen when the dog left?'

'The prow will then have been thrown more upwards, and the flight rendered gradually ascending again. Moreover, as the helm was free, the course must inevitably follow the wind. The engine had some eight more hours to run – so it must have alighted well inland in South Norway. Follow on! We'll track it yet!'

There was still some ground for hope. Within an hour we had renewed our pursuit, via Lemvig across to Christiansund. Everywhere the scent was fresh and strong. Look-out men had heard strange noises in the sky: boatmen had seen a strange monster flying seaward. And when we reached the Norwegian coast we heard a strange story come down from the hills, that an unknown visitor had come into a distant valley with her leg broken, but how or whence, being a foreigner, she could not explain. The mountain track thither was declared impassable – but we were not to be stayed now. Guidance was found at a fancy price – 500 kroner to the man who could lead us to the Horndal Valley – and through weary days and bitter nights we forced our way to the distant valley.

Our provisions were running out, and we were half-dead with the piercing cold: but hope kept us steadfast. And at length we knew we had succeeded – for of a sudden we found that Carlo had deserted us. His deep voice was presently heard at no great distance – and shortly afterwards our eye confirmed that our darling was safe.

She was standing in the open doorway of a grass-thatched wooden house, leaning on a stick, but with a flush of health on her cheek and with a gleam in her eyes that told us all was well.

She had alighted hard by in a valley five weeks before, but in her eagerness to jump out became involved in part of the machinery still in motion, and one of the bones in the left ankle had been fractured. It was not serious, and was now practically whole again.

She was standing in the open doorway of a grass-thatched wooden house, leaning on a stick.

Only when he had heard all her story did Broughton ask the question which was only less important to him than the well-being of Mabel herself: 'What happened to it – what became of it?'

'As soon as I got out it rose again. It is caught somewhere among those awful pinnacles there against the sky.'

We knew those towering pinnacles through which we had fought our way to reach her. Shading our eyes we thought we could now and again catch some vague object among their dizzy heights, flapping in the wind.

'There let it lie for ever,' he said at length, 'now that you are safe!'

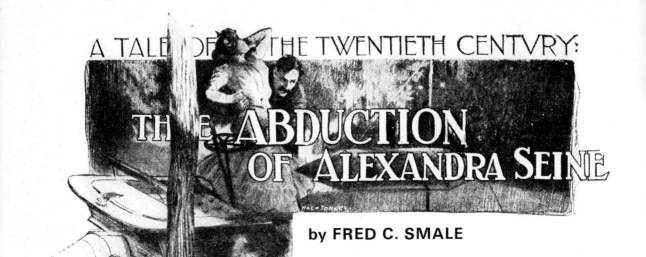

A TALE OF THE TWENTIETH CENTVRY:

THE ABDUCTION OF ALEXANDRA SEINE

by FRED C. SMALE

'EIGHO, this is gruesome work,' exclaimed Bowden Snell, as he leaned back in his old Victorian chair and placed a cocaine lozenge in his mouth.

A particularly atrocious crime had been committeed that morning in the suburb of Slough, and Snell, in his capacity of graphist to the *Hourly Flash,* had been sent to procure a record of it by means of the Antegraph. He had the advantage of possessing a good instrument, and five minutes had sufficed to obtain good retrospective views of the crime, from the first frown of the murderer to the last dying throe of the victim. He was now developing the film in his room at the *Flash* office, and the aerocar which had brought him was still outside the large bay window swinging gently to and fro at its moorings in the summer breeze.

It was now sixteen o'clock, and the pictures were needed for the seventeen o'clock edition. The murderer had been caught, of course: a constable, equipped with collapsible wings, had swooped down on the guilty ruffian ere he had reached Windsor, whither he was making, doubtless with the intention of taking an aerocar from the rank on Castle Hill.

Bowden Snell was not young, being over fifty, and the more rapid methods of the times made it difficult for him to compete with younger men: the *Flash* retained him chiefly for his extensive knowledge of the great province of London. His films completed, Snell mechanically pressed a button in the wall beside him, and commenced to apply himself voraciously to the resulting salmon cutlets. But he had scarcely eaten a mouthful when the room was suddenly darkened by the apparition of a second aerocar of strange old-fashioned construction, which bumped clumsily against Snell's own machine, and ultimately drew up at the window. Immediately a young man, clad in white from head to foot, leaped into the room. His face was brown with exposure to the sun, and he looked anxious and travel-worn.

'Arbuthnot! What on earth –?'

'Give me a bite of something, for Heaven's sake: I'm famished.'

The other turned to the wall and hurriedly pressed a number of buttons.

'Steady, I say,' said the young man. 'Roast turkey, cold salad, fried soles, Burgundy – bit of a mixture, eh?'

The elder man checked himself. 'But how is it you are here? I thought you were in Japan, developing that part of the empire?'

'Mr Snell, I am in great trouble.'

'Hum, it hasn't affected your appetite!'

'Perhaps not; but I can tell you the air of the Himalayas is pretty keen, at least I found it so this morning as I came through . . . Listen, I took with me to Japan two telepathic instruments.'

'Ha, a lady's whim, eh,?'

'Something of my own idea as well,' the young man flushed. 'You see, one can't run home here to England every few weeks, and Ally and I thought it would be nice to sit and talk to each other sometimes. Now, this morning a strange thing happened. You must understand I have one instrument upstairs and the other down in the sitting-room: it isn't always so easy to hit the mark in Japan, you know, owing to the earthquakes, so that when Ally missed one with a message the chances were that she would hit the other.'

'I see.'

'Well, I was sitting down this morning having a smoke after the day's work – it was evening there, of course – when the signal of the instrument clicked, and I heard my dar – Ally's voice, I mean, in great distress, calling "Help, help, Jack! I am being carried away" – then silence. I rushed upstairs to the other instrument, thinking it might catch something the other missed, but I heard nothing more, though I shouted continually.'

'Shouting's never any good: only rattles the mechanism. You took the direction?'

'Due west, two degrees from normal.'

The other took a scrap of paper and made a few rapid calculations. 'She must have been in the air, then.'

'That's how I worked it out. Three hundred feet from the ground, and fifty miles south of Greenwich.'

'About that,' Snell agreed. 'Well, what are you going to do, and what do you want of me?'

'I thought of you immediately, so, placing a few food-pellets in my pocket, I jumped on my machine and came away just as I was. Luckily my aerocar was fully charged – but it took me sixteen hours to do the journey: I can't afford a new machine. I've come to you as my father's friend – and because you know London Province better than any man: I want you to find Ally.'

The other nodded. 'What is she like, to begin with?'

The young man took a small case from his breast-pocket: applying his eye to the aperture and pressing the knob, Snell watched a brief graphilm of a remarkably pretty girl.

He returned it to Arbuthnot with a smile. 'Well, now we know what we're hunting for, we can start hunting.'

'But we have no clue where to look!'

'Hush, let me think . . .' Snell passed his hand over his forehead, then, stepping across the room, he pressed a knob in the wall, causing a little shutter to fall.

'What place?' asked a faint voice.

'The whole of East London, from Greenwich to St Pauls.'

'It's rather dark, but I'll try.'

The two men applied their eyes to the circular orifices. 'Do you see anything?' asked Arbuthnot, presently.

'Only the usual crowd of aerocars above, and athletes walking in the streets below. I see nothing suspicious. Wait – no, only some air-sailors drinking absinthe. You there?' he called. 'Give me a line due east of Greenwich straight to the sea.'

'Apparatus only reaches Swanley: line broken down.'

'When will they perfect these things!' exclaimed Arbuthnot impatiently, then suddenly added 'There she is!'

'You are sure it is she?'

'Quite sure – but who is the man with her, I wonder?'

'Eagle Malvowley – I might have guessed,' cried Snell. 'He must be taking her to his castle in the Balkans. We must follow at once.

'I don't understand. There is open sea beneath them, yet the operator told us –'

'You there?' came the voice. 'The instrument is out of order. By mistake I started you from the French end: you have checked it in mid-Channel.'

'Ah, that explains it,' said Snell. 'But why are they stationary?'

'I don't know, but it gives us a chance to overtake them. Come, let us away!'

'My machine,' said Snell, 'it is the swifter.'

With a whiz and a flutter they rose through the cool evening air, and, after soaring undecidedly over the ancient dome of St Pauls, sped off to the east. The air was full of business cars, rising in shoals from the heart of the province only to drop in various suburbs. Once away from the centre, however, the travellers were able to put on full speed, and in a few minutes the silvery gleam of the Channel appeared in sight.

They searched the air with strained eyes as they sped along: but beyond the usual Continental and Far East cars, they saw nothing of consequence. As they neared the sea they decided to descend, and dropped lightly at the very water's edge, on a secluded beach

They rose over the dome of St. Paul's and sped away in an easterly direction.

between Dover and Folkestone. They stepped out
on the yielding sand, and stood by the rippling
waves. A huge full moon was just appearing above
the horizon. Far above them a few aerocars wafted
their way towards their various destinations, and
the alert customs officers in their crimson-painted
machines flitted restlessly hither and thither.

'If he has crossed the Channel, we shall never
find him. We are beaten!'

'Wait,' said Snell, narrowly scanning an ap-
proaching car. 'There's Jim Travers of the *Minute
Gun*. Above there, Travers!' he shouted lustily.

'Hello, Snell,' came the reply, 'what's amiss?'
The car swooped gracefully to within a few yards
of their heads.

'Have you seen Eagle Malvowley in your
travels?'

'Passed him just half way across. He had a break-
down – jammed lever, I fancy – and is fluttering
about like a wounded gull.'

'Anyone with him?'

'Couldn't see, too dark.'

But with a shout of thanks, Snell and Arbuthnot were already soaring over the sea. 'Lucky I saw him – been over to Baden for the afternoon's races, I dare say,' said Snell. But Arbuthnot's attention was concentrated on the night sky ahead. Suddenly he grasped Snell's arm.

Snell nodded, and with a skilfully executed upward swoop he guided the machine to within a dozen yards of the apparently uncontrollable fugitive car, in which a slight tall man with a dark saturnine countenance was uttering vicious oaths while he hammered spitefully at some part of the machinery. The beloved object of their search lay on the bottom of the machine, to all appearance lifeless.

Malvowley was so engrossed in his task that he had not noticed the approach of his pursuers, but a fierce hail from Arbuthnot made him leap up. With an execration he picked up a ball-shaped object and hurled it at his interrupters, but in his sudden surprise he missed his aim. Snell hastily seized a lever to send the car some fifty feet above Malvowley's.

'Rippite bomb,' he exclaimed as the missile struck the water below and burst with the soft seductive whirr of that deadly explosive.

'You are helpless, Malvowley,' cried Arbuthnot. 'Hand over Miss Seine at once.'

'Come and take her – if you can. I shan't miss you a second time.'

'We must board him – it's our only chance,' said Snell. 'If he once gets his machine running again, he will be the other side of Europe in five minutes. She's a racer, built for last year's America Cup. I'll swoop as close as I can, and you must leap for it.'

'I'll try it. If I miss, you must descend on the chance of picking me up.' The aerocar swooped down. With a fast-beating heart Arbuthnot hurled himself into the car, knocking the surprised Malvowley into a corner where he lay momentarily stunned. With lightning movements the young man seized the unconscious girl in his arms and passed her over to Snell, who stood ready to receive her. Arbuthnot had scarcely time to leap back after, when Malvowley recovered himself and, with horrible oaths, rushed to the side of his car.

'Curse you!' he shrieked. 'I'll wreck you – I'll send you all to eternity!'

'Up – up – quick! Another bomb!'

They rose with sickening speed, while Malvowley, foaming with demoniacal rage, hurled another deadly missile up after them. They were too quick, however, and the bomb fell back again onto his own car. As the ball touched the car it exploded: the detonation scattered the machine and its unhappy occupant into a million fragments.

Some of the wreckage struck the victors as they still soared upwards, but they were rising too rapidly to suffer any injury. When at last, pale and trembling, they found courage to look down, only a few pieces of floating wood and aluminium far below remained as witnesses of Eagle Malvowley's fearful end.

The bomb fell back on Malvowley's own car, scattering the machine into a million fragments.

91

5 'I was as God!'

Tales of men with strange powers...
as yet unknown to science

The Charlatan *(Frank Harris, 1902)*

The Shadow & the Flash *(Jack London, 1906)*

The Man who meddled with Eternity *(E. Tickner-Edwardes, 1901)*

Acquisitiveness (desire to possess) was somewhere near the ears. Inhabitiveness (love for home or country) was at the back of the skull. Amativeness (the desire to caress and fondle) was down at the bottom of the neck conveniently adjacent to philoprogenitiveness (desire to reproduce one's kind) . . .

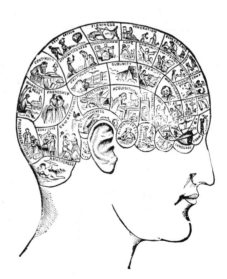

It was simply a matter of feeling the bumps on the head. Before dinner you could establish that Charles was alimentive: after dinner he became philoprogenitive unless someone kept a sharp eye on him. The dashing Captain was gallantly inhabitive and cousin Bella distinctly more amative than was proper . . . It was a parlour game conducive of great

mirth, but it was more: it made you realise what a truly wonderful thing was the human mind.

Sometimes at the dinner table there would be a guest — perhaps an embarrassing foreigner with a black beard and a guttural accent — who would hold forth about less mirthful discoveries in the human mind. He

might even speak (until a reproachful glance from his host hinted that such topics were best postponed till the ladies had left the menfolk to their brandy and cigars) of Doctor Freud in Vienna who had discovered that the undercurrents of man's mind were really rather nasty. That didn't matter so much — hadn't one always suspected something of the sort? — but what was worse was that the Doctor claimed that the under-currents of a woman's mind were little or no better. Even the suffragettes weren't too happy about carrying equality this far.

It was a pleasant relief to turn to the activities of the societies for Psychical Research now to be found in most countries. The British society had been founded in 1882 and was a thoroughly respectable organisation — some would say too respectable. Its members made remarkable discoveries. Gilbert Murray, the noted Greek scholar, con-ducted amazing experiments in telepathy. William James, the most eminent psychologist of his day, vouched for extraordinary medium-istic phenomena. They showed beyond dispute that the human mind possessed resources which far exceeded those which were used in daily life. What's more, it seemed that these powers did not necessarily cease even with death. Ever since the Fox sisters had started the spiritualist cult in 1848, tables had been rapping out messages some of which seemed to emanate from another world.

Was that world the spirit world? Then, as now, the average citizen didn't know what to believe. Many claimants to spiritualist powers were exposed as frauds: but a few remained to perplex. Daniel Dunglass Home, for example, was never exposed — never even came near to being exposed — throughout his long career. Scottish by birth, brought up in America, Home early revealed a remarkable skill in the traditional psychic feat of making furniture rise from the floor. Later he added levitation of his own body to his repertoire. He spent his life exhibiting his powers, always in the best society, meeting a great many of the famous people of his day. Robert Browning loathed him and assailed him in *Mr Sludge the Medium*, but the Emperor of France was impressed when Home raised a vast palatial dining-table into the air, caused hands to materialise and sign Napoleon's autograph.

Unlike most mediums, Home was calm, relaxed, respectable, and his seances always dignified. Sometimes he seemed to be in some kind of trance, at others he seemed in no way different from his usual self: either way, phenomena might or might not occur. The greater number of his sittings took place in full light, surrounded by strangers, in public rooms.

HOME LEVITATING The American spiritualist Daniel Dunglass Home, though relentlessly pursued by would-be exposers, was never detected in any imposture or trick. His feats of levitation, such as this ascent in London depicted in Figuier's 'Les Mysteres de la Science', have never been satisfactorily explained by critics.

His success aroused hostility in some, bafflement in others. It was frustrating for those who could not account for his phenomena to be continually confronted with the mystery. Yet he himself was baffled too. 'I have not the slightest power over these manifestations, either to bring them on, or send them away. What may be the peculiar laws under which they have developed in my person, I know no more than others. Some of the phenomena are noble and elevated, others are grotesque. For this I am not responsible. I solemnly swear that I do not produce the phenomena, or in any way whatever aid in producing them.'

Well then. if Home were honest and his powers genuine, if any family party could summon spirits from the vasty deep, what limit was there to the potential of the human mind? The average citizen — and the writers who catered for his entertainment — were ready to jump all barriers, cross all frontiers, accept all miracles.

A CHARLATAN

by FRANK HARRIS

ORTIMER was always rather peculiar. He and I were at school together, and about the same age, and so saw a good deal of each other. He was unlike other boys – strangely proud and sensitive. He never went in much for games, and the time hung heavy on his hands till to my surprise he began to take up chemistry, and was always in and out of the laboratory. Our Science master was inordinately proud of having secured a willing student, and the two became inseparable. I saw less and less of Mortimer, but our friendship continued – for with all his pride he was gentle and affectionate.

In October 1882 I went to Balliol, and Mortimer came up to Oxford in the following May. Here he went in for abstruse, visionary studies: interesting, if you like, but vague and unprofitable. Sometimes he would look me up and have a talk. Now and again he spoke of his ambitions, or rather of his hopes: when you come to deal with the mysteries, hopes are as much as you can have.

In due time I took my degree, came to London and was called to the Bar. I lost sight of Mortimer completely, and for years scarcely heard of him. I knew in a vague way that he had gone down to his people in Wales, and been a great disappointment to them. He would not enter any of the professions, nor marry, nor take to himself any of the usual burdens of life. He grew more and more solitary, and at last went and built himself a cottage and a laboratory on the coast of Cardigan Bay, with money left to him by his mother, and there spent some of the best years of his life, more like a hermit than a reasonable human being.

Years passed before I heard of Mortimer again. He was lecturing in London and the provinces, and scraps of his talk came to me now and then, filtered through the daily papers. One or two phrases that escaped the mangling of the reporters interested me: 'Laws of nature and ideas in the mind suppose each other as eyes suppose light . . . Spiritual forces can be measured as easily as mechanical forces, and will be found more efficient.'

People thought him mad: he pretended to be able to work miracles, they said, and told wild stories that I had neither the time nor the inclination to investigate. Mortimer was the last person in the world, I thought, to try to impose on any one. I was dumbfounded when news came of the scandal at Birmingham – Mortimer accused of cheating and swindling. Impossible! In my indignation I tore up the paper that held the news and pitched it out of my brougham window. That very afternoon Mortimer came to my office.

He had changed greatly. The light brown hair had turned grey; the slight figure had lost its spring; the hands twined nervously. He threw himself into my armchair with a sigh: then suddenly sprang up in the old abrupt way. 'I want your judgment of me, and no one else's!'

He was so nervous and excited that I humoured him. I sent my clerk away, filled my pipe, drew up another chair, and said 'Go ahead.' I was as eager as a girl to hear his story.

'You know,' he began, 'I worked at science at Winchester. I did a good deal there. At Oxford I did a lot of gas analysis and some physics; then I went over to Heidelberg and spent four or five years with Bunsen. Then I went down to Wales and started my chemical laboratory. I made some curious discoveries: I found very soon that one can fuse and mix bodies without regard for their different atomic weights. If they refuse to mix, you heat them, or pass an electric spark through them, and they unite at once. And then I found that when I had no electricity, I could mix them by personal magnetism, if virtue sufficient were in me. You shrug your shoulders and don't believe me: but it is true nevertheless.

'At length I resolved to do something that would convince you sceptics. I hoped to prove that matter is not dead: that stones and metals are endowed with sensation and will. I determined to fuse metals together in such a way that they would do my bidding: that the mass would come when I asked it to come, go when I told it to go, stand still when I bade it stand still, and so prove that the spirit

of man is that of God, and rules throughout creation.' He looked up suddenly; but I was listening enthralled – his enthusiasm had infected me. 'I went to work to fuse my metals – first three, then nine. I failed absolutely. At length I fused seven metals, because 7 was a sacred number to men in the past, and lo! I succeeded at once beyond all hope. I made a large mould of the best fireclay to resist heat – a perfect sphere, 49 inches in diameter – 7 times 7, you know – then poured in my seven metals. The next morning, when the metal had had time to cool, I went back, and there was the mould cracked and broken. I was hideously disappointed.

'I had made the mould hollow, in order to get a skin of metal an inch thick, for otherwise the mass would have been unwieldy. Well, I found the mould cracked and gaping, and when I broke it away, out rolled a ball, wobbling and imperfect instead of my perfect sphere. At first I was in despair, and then puzzled. The colour of the thing was superb; it had the play and light on it of steel, and the glow of gold. But it was not round. Then the truth came to me in a flash: I saw that it was the shape of the earth – flattened at both poles, bulged at the equator. The laws that made the world had made my sphere – and I knew I had succeeded. For I called the ball and it rolled and wobbled towards me, and I sent it away and it rolled away, and I told it to stop and it stood still – I was as God!

'It drove me nearly mad. For the curious part of the matter is that though I went to sleep that night with the magic ball by my bedside, exultant and content, and awoke refreshed and happy, yet in the morning I had lost my power. It was heartbreaking. I spoke to the ball and it did not respond. After that one moment of power, I had weeks of disappointment and doubt – yes, doubt, for in time I even came to doubt whether my success had not been a deception of fevered senses. At length I put the ball out of my mind and went on with some other work: and suddenly one day I found I had regained my power over the ball and could make it do whatever I wanted. I called it up the stairs after me, and then out on the beach, and I could have knelt and kissed the mark it left on the sand.

'Months passed, and years, and I got no further. Sometimes for days I had control of the ball, then of a sudden the power would leave me and I was plunged into hell. Then again a change would come, and I was master again. One thing upheld me. It seemed to me that gradually I was getting more and more control over my strange companion; the periods in which it disobeyed me grew shorter and shorter.

'But the imperfect tortured me, and the alternations of hope and fear broke down my health. I grew frightened of myself, and was afraid, too, to wait too long lest my secret should perish with me. With this thought in my head, I came up to London and began to lecture. The change did my health good, and I got to love the work. And when I told them from the platform that I would give them a proof of my theories, people believed me who would not otherwise

I called the ball and it rolled and wobbled towards me, and I sent it away and it rolled away and I told it to stop and it stood still.

99

have believed my teaching, nor even have cared to listen to it. Like children, they were pleased with the puzzle and nothing more. The secret of life which I had discovered did not interest them: it was the miracle they had come to see.

'One night I was tired, and the ball responded badly – scarcely moved at all, in fact – and the people laughed and hooted, and some wanted their money back: they sickened me with disappointment, and afterwards that impression grew upon me and the more I thought of it the more frightened I became. The whole of my teaching was endangered because the visible proof was not always with me. And so temptation came to me. I cut an opening in the ball, and got a little boy who could enter it and move it as he liked from the inside. It took me only a week or so to construct the mechanism. You disapprove, I see: but think, after all, it was only making certain what was usual and ordinary.

'Besides, I hardly ever employed my boy – my word of honour – he was not necessary. His mere presence gave me confidence, and I went on for weeks successfully. I lectured throughout the country without using the boy at all.

'It was at Manchester that I first noticed a man in the audience who sat there sneering disbelief at me while I talked. I could see envy and hatred in his eyes, and I grew afraid of him. His influence was evil, and my second night at Manchester I put Walter in the ball. I had lost confidence . . . From that day on I used the boy occasionally, for the evil face followed me all over the country – the same face in every audience, and I grew to loathe it.

'I was lecturing at Birmingham, I remember, when I noticed that man before me in the fifth row, and I grew cold with fear. But the people were enthusiastic, and when at the end I told the ball to come to me and it came, I was quite confident and happy. But when I looked out over the audience in triumph I noticed the man with the evil face had got up in his place to watch the ball; in half a minute he sat down again with a grin, as if he had solved the riddle – the poor fool!

'The next afternoon my boy asked me for the evening off – he wanted to visit his mother. But I said "No, Walter, I am not quite well, and I shall be afraid without you."

'He looked at me a little sullenly. "You don't need me, Professor. You know the ball goes just as well without me: it always starts before I even put my weight on the bar."

'But I insisted that he should be there, and opened my second lecture with the boy in the sphere. The hall was crowded, and the people more enthusiastic than ever: but when I called the ball to me it would scarcely move. I trembled, fearing that Walter was disobedient. In the audience there were murmurs of discontent.

'Suddenly the man with the evil face rose. "Ladies and gentlemen, I have followed these lectures for weeks. That man is an imposter. His trick is a swindle and a cheat." The next moment he was beside me on the stage. He declared there must be a young boy or girl in the ball to move it, and he dared me to let him examine the ball and show what he called the fact.

'I looked at him. "What does the fact prove? Doesn't the lesson remain whether the ball stands still or moves?"

'He laughed in my face. "Who cares for your lesson or your teaching? The thing we want to know is whether you can make dead metal move; you can take your teaching where you like. Is there anyone inside that ball or not – that's what we want to know."

'Even as I withstood him I noticed that all were on his side and against me, and because they rejected my teaching, hatred of them overcame me, and contempt. "What if there is a boy in the ball?"

'He shouted in triumph. "I knew it was a boy! He has confessed!"

'I can't tell all they said and did in their rage, but at last they gave me a pen and ink and told me to write the admission that there was a boy inside the ball, and that I had cheated them, or else they would break open the ball and see for themselves.

'I was tired to death, and my soul was filled with contempt of them and loathing; and at last I signed the paper admitting I was a cheat; and they jeered and spat on me, and crowed that Birmingham was too wise to be taken in by my tricks, and went away sneering and triumphant.

'I sat on the platform deserted and alone, shamed to the soul; my life in ruins about me. Suddenly a door at the right of the stage opened, and little Walter came in. When he saw me he hesitated.

' "I'm sorry, Professor," he said, hanging his head. "I did so want to see my mother. But the ball moved, didn't it, just the same?"

' "You were not in the ball, then, Walter?"

'He answered, looking at me in astonishment: "No, Professor, I was not in the ball. I have only just come back." '

THE SHADOW AND THE FLASH

by JACK LONDON

HEN I look back, I realise what a peculiar friendship it was. First, Lloyd Inwood, tall, slender, nervous, dark: then Paul Tichlorne, tall, slender, nervous and blond. Each was the replica of the other in everything except colour. Outside this, they were as alike as two peas. Both were high-strung, prone to excessive tension and over-endurance, and they lived constantly at concert pitch.

But there was a trio involved in this remarkable friendship, and the third was short and fat and chunky and lazy, and, loth to say, it was I. Paul and Lloyd seemed born to rivalry with each other, and I to be peacemaker between them. We grew up together, the three of us, and full often have I received the angry blows each intended for the other. They were always competing, striving to outdo each other, and when entered upon some such struggle there was no limit either to their endeavours or passions.

When Paul Tichlorne entered college he let it be generally understood that he was going in for the social sciences. Lloyd Inwood elected to take the same course. But Paul had it secretly in mind all the time to specialise on chemistry, and at the last moment he changed over. Lloyd at once followed Paul's lead. Their rivalry soon became a noted thing throughout the university. Each was a spur to the other, and they went into chemistry deeper than did ever students before – so deep, in fact, that, ere they took their degrees, they could have stumped any prof in the institution save the head – and him even they puzzled more than once. Lloyd's discovery of the 'death bacillus' of the sea-toad sent his name and that of the university ringing round the world: nor was Paul a whit behind when he succeeded in his startling experiments on the processes of fertilisation of marine life.

It was at my home, after they had taken their degrees and dropped out of the world's sight, that the beginning of the end came to pass.

k here, Paul, you'll keep out
his if you know what's good
you.

Both were men of means, with little inclination and no necessity for professional life. My friendship and their mutual animosity were the two things that linked them. While they were often at my place, they made it a fastidious point to avoid each other, though it was inevitable that they should come upon each other occasionally.

On the day I have in recollection, I had left Paul mooning in my study over a scientific review and was out among my roses when Lloyd arrived. For some reason, as I worked, with Lloyd nervously following me about, we got to talking about invisibility: Lloyd contended that a perfectly black object would elude and defy the acutest vision. 'Colour is a sensation, it has no objective reality. Without light, we can see neither colours nor objects themselves. All objects are black in the dark, and it is impossible to see them.'

'But we see black objects in daylight.'

'That's because they are not perfectly black. With the right pigments, an absolutely black paint could be produced which would render invisible whatever it was applied to . . . With such a paint, I would have the world at my feet. The secrets of kings and courts would be mine, the machinations of diplomats, the play of tricksters, the plans of corporations! I could become the greatest power in the world! and I –' He broke off shortly; then added: 'Well, I have begun my experiments, and I don't mind telling you that I'm right in line for it.'

A sneering laugh from the doorway startled us. Paul Tichlorne stood there, a smile of mockery on his lips. 'My dear Lloyd, you forget – the shadow!'

'I can carry a sunshade, you know!'

'No, you will always fetch up against your shadow, you can't get away from it. Now, I should go on the very opposite tack.'

'Transparency? It can't be achieved!'

'Oh no, of course not.' And Paul shrugged his shoulders and strolled away.

That was the beginning of it. Both men attacked the problem with all their tremendous energy, and with a bitterness which made me tremble for the success of either. Each trusted me, and in the weeks of experiment that followed I was made a party to both sides, never conveying to one the slightest hint of the other's progress, and they respected me for the seal I put on my lips.

I visited Lloyd's laboratory a number of times, and found him always deep in his search after absolute black. Lamp-blacks, tars, carbonised vegetable matters, soots of oil and fats – he was trying everything: one, I remember, I could hardly see – just to look at it gave me a blurring sensation which remained even when I rubbed my eyes. 'That,' Lloyd said, 'is the blackest black any mortal ever looked upon. But just you wait, and I'll have a black so black that no mortal will be able to look upon it – and see it!'

Paul, on the other hand, I found plunged as deeply into the study of light polarisation, diffraction and interference, single and double refraction, and all manner of strange organic compounds.

'Transparency: a state of body which allows all rays of light to pass through – that's what I am seeking. Such a body will cast no shadow and, since it reflects no light, it will also be invisible.'

We were standing by the window. Paul was engaged in polishing a number of lenses. Suddenly he said 'Oh, I've dropped one! Stick your head out, old man, and see where it went to.'

Out I started to thrust my head, but a sharp blow on my head caused me to recoil. I rubbed my bruised brow and turned to Paul, who was laughing gleefully. 'Why don't you investigate?' he asked.

I stretched forth my hand and felt a hard object, smooth and cool and flat, which my touch, out of its experience, told me to be glass. But I could see positively nothing.

'White quartose sand – sodic carbonate – slaked lime – cullet – manganese peroxide – the finest plate-glass in the world. You can't see it till you run your head against it – but certain elements, in themselves opaque, can be compounded to give a resultant body which is transparent. Well, I purpose to find the proper reagents which, acting upon a living organism, will produce a similar result.'

A few weeks later I went shooting with Paul. He had been promising me for some time that I should have the pleasure of shooting over the most wonderful dog that ever man shot over – but on the morning in question there was no dog in evidence. 'Don't see him about,' Paul remarked unconcernedly, and we set off across the fields.

I could not imagine at the time what was ailing me, but my nerves seemed to be all awry. Strange sounds disturbed me. At times I heard the swish-swish of grass being pushed aside, and once I heard the eager whine of a dog apparently from within a couple of feet of me: but on looking about me I saw nothing. Paul laughed loud and long. 'What did I tell you – the most wonderful dog, eh? Here, give me your fist.' And he rubbed my hand over the cold nose and jowls of a dog. And a dog it certainly was, though I could see nothing: it had the shape and the smooth, short coat of a pointer.

Paul put a collar about the animal's neck, and tied his handkerchief to its tail. And then was vouchsafed us the remarkable sight of an empty collar and a waving handkerchief cavorting over the fields. The only further sign was an occasional vari-coloured flash of light – the one thing, Paul confessed, which he had not anticipated. 'They are produced by refraction of light, and I am afraid they are the penalty I must pay for transparency. I escaped Lloyd's shadow only to fetch up against the rainbow flash.'

While Paul was thus mastering the problem of invisibility in his way, Lloyd was pursuing his own course no less successfully. I went over to his laboratory in answer to an invitation: conceive of my surprise when I turned the corner of the path to find that the building had utterly vanished. I started to walk across what had once been its site. 'This,' I said to myself, 'should be where the doorstep was'

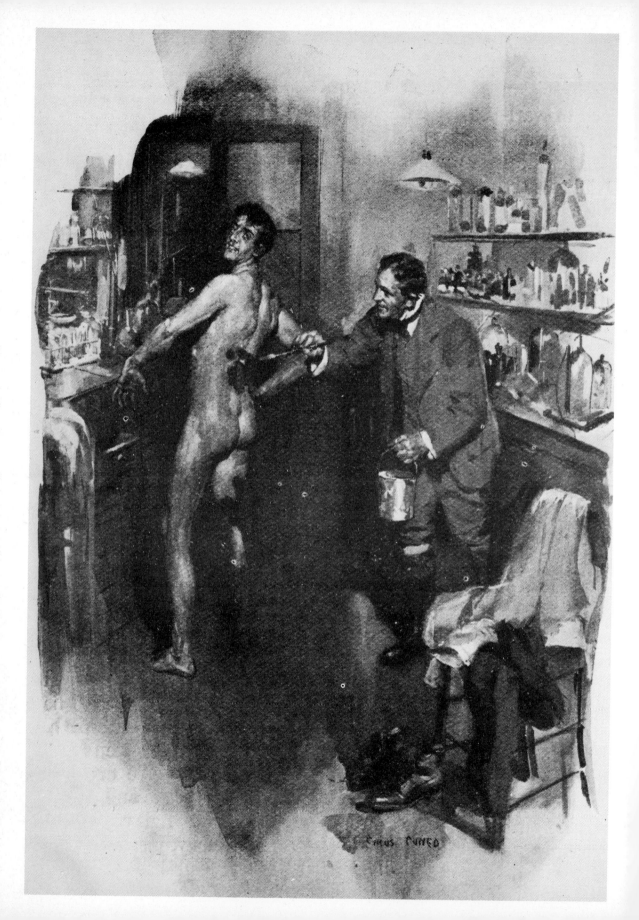

and barely were the words uttered when I stubbed my toe on some obstacle, pitched forward, and butted my head into something which certainly *felt* like a door. I found a knob and turned it: at once the whole interior of the laboratory impinged upon my vision.

'What do you think of it, eh?' Lloyd asked, wringing my hand. 'I slapped a couple of coats of absolute black on the outside yesterday afternoon, to see how it worked.'

While he talked, he began to strip, and when he stood naked before me, he thrust a pot and brush into my hand. 'Here, give me a coat of this.'

It was an oily, shellac-like stuff which spread quickly and easily over the skin and dried immediately.

'Merely preliminary,' he explained. 'Now for the real thing.'

I picked up another pot he indicated, but could see nothing inside it.

'Stick your finger in it.'

I obeyed, and was aware of a sensation of cool moistness. On withdrawing my hand I glanced at my forefinger, but it had disappeared. To all appearances I had been shorn of a finger, nor could I get any visual impression of it till I held it under the skylight and saw its shadow on the floor.

Lloyd chuckled. 'Now spread it on, and keep your eyes open.'

I dipped the brush into the seemingly empty pot, and gave him a long stroke across the chest. The living flesh disappeared. I covered his right leg, and he was as a one-legged man defying all laws of gravitation. And so, stroke by stroke, I painted him into nothingness. It was a creepy experience, and I was glad when naught remained but his burning black eyes, poised apparently unsupported in mid-air. 'A fine spray with an air-brush, and presto, I am not!'

This accomplished, he asked 'Now tell me what you can see.'

'In the first place, I cannot see you. You cannot escape your shadow, but that was to be expected. When you pass between my eye and an object, the object disappears – but it's more as though my eyes had blurred. When you move rapidly, I experience a bewildering succession of blurs.'

'Have you any other warnings of my presence?'

'When you are near me, I seem to feel the loom of your body – but it is all very vague and intangible.'

Long we talked, that last morning in his laboratory: and when I turned to go, he put his unseen hand in mine with nervous grip: 'Now I shall conquer the world!' I did not dare tell him of Paul's equal success.

At home I found a note from Paul, asking me to visit him. When I arrived, Paul called me from the tennis-court, and I went over. But the court was empty. Then, as I stood there, a tennis-ball struck me on the arm, and as I turned about, another whizzed past my ear. For aught I could see of my assailant, they came whirling at me from out of space, and right well was I peppered. But then I realised the

covered his right leg, and he was as a one-legged man defying all laws of gravitation.

I could do nothing, so I sat up, fascinated and powerless, and watched the struggle.

situation. Seizing a racquet and keeping my eyes open, I quickly saw a rainbow flash darting over the ground. I went after it, and when I had laid the racquet on it for half-a-dozen stout blows, Paul's voice rang out. 'Enough! Stop, you're landing on my naked skin, you know!'

A few minutes later we were playing tennis – a handicap on my part, for I had no knowledge of his position save when the angles between himself, the sun and me were in proper conjunction. Then he flashed, and only then.

But in the midst of our play I felt a sudden strange sensation, such as I had experienced that very morning. The next moment, close to the net, I saw a ball rebound in mid-air and empty space, and at the same instance, a score of feet away, Paul emit a rainbow flash. It could not be he from whom the ball had rebounded, and I realised that Lloyd had come upon the scene. To make sure, I looked for his shadow, and there it was, a shapeless blotch the girth of his body (the sun was overhead) moving along the ground. I remembered his threat, and felt sure that all the long years of rivalry were about to culminate in hideous battle.

I cried a warning to Paul, and heard a snarl as of a wild beast. I saw the dark blotch move swiftly across the court, and a brilliant burst of vari-coloured light moving with equal swiftness to meet it; and then shadow and flash came together, and there was the sound of unseen blows. The net was down before my frightened eyes. I sprang towards the fighters, but an unseen blow sent me staggering back. 'You keep out of this, old man,' I heard the voice of Lloyd Inwood from out of the emptiness, and Paul's voice echoed 'Yes, we've had enough of peacemaking!'

I could do nothing, so I sat up, fascinated and powerless, and watched the struggle. The noonday sun beat down with dazzling brightness on the naked tennis court. And it *was* naked. All I could see was the blotch of shadow and the rainbow flashes, the dust rising from the invisible feet, the earth tearing up from beneath the straining foot-grips, and the wire screen bulge once or twice as their bodies were hurled against it. That was all, and after a time even that ceased. There were no more flashes, and the shadow had become stationary.

The secrets of their discoveries died with them, both laboratories being destroyed by grief-stricken relatives. As for myself, I no longer care for chemical research. I have returned to my roses. Nature's colours are good enough for me.

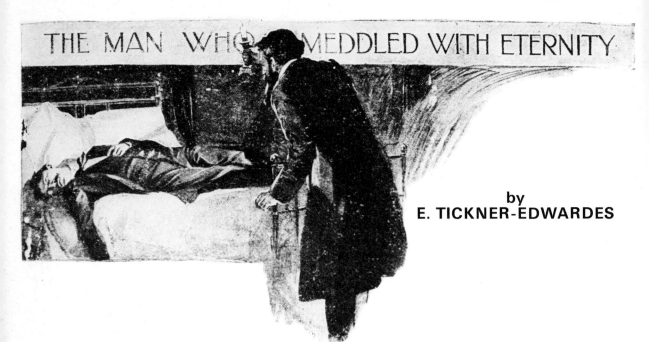

THE MAN WHO MEDDLED WITH ETERNITY

by
E. TICKNER-EDWARDES

UTE Walton? The luckiest beggar on the face of the earth!'

The speaker was a tall bronzed man, and the words were uttered so vehemently that everyone at Sir James Banyard's end of the table turned to him in surprise.

Dinner was over; the ladies were gone; and the talk, as usual at Sir James' cosy little medico-scientific reunions, had drifted into discussion of new theories – and the men who propounded those theories. Someone had mentioned Walton's name – and thereby provoked this sudden exclamation.

'I knew him well,' the stranger continued. 'I knew his wife, too, long before she was Mrs Walton.'

'Then, Gallier, you can tell us about the lady. Clinthorpe here was saying she was the most beautiful woman he ever beheld.'

Gallier spoke almost below his breath. 'Yes, she *is* beautiful: or was – for it is a good ten years since I saw her. I have been all over the world since then, and I had no idea that Bute Walton was anything more than an obscure country practitioner. So he is now a famous consultant, is he? What is his subject?'

Clinthorpe laughed. 'You don't seem to know much about our new celebrity, yet you call him the luckiest beggar on earth. Perhaps you had him in mind only as the fortunate possessor of the lady?'

No one could have been more astounded than little Clinthorpe when he found himself suddenly seized by the collar. But before a hand could be raised to separate them, Gallier had released his hold. 'I ask your pardon. I have lived so long among savages that I have forgotten I was ever bred a gentleman. Forgive me.'

Clinthorpe extended his hand to close the incident, and Sir James proposed that they join the ladies. But Stephen Gallier, muttering some clumsy excuse, took his departure at once.

Out in the street, he found his footsteps turning, not towards his hotel, but into Grosvenor Crescent: he stood for a long while in the quiet night, staring up at the windows of a great mansion there. For the first time in years, it seemed, he had allowed his thoughts to drift from nigger-doctoring and gold-prospecting in the African swamps. 'Lettie Carol, Lettie Carol! How long it seems since you and I were splitting bandages together and talking nonsense. But you never understood – Ah, will there never come a time when I can forget? What a cursed fool I was to come back!'

Suddenly his thoughts were disturbed by the arrival of a smart carriage which drew up at the door. The footman opened the door, a lady descended: Lettie Walton. He saw her start – her look of recognition.

'Lettie, Lettie – do you remember me, after all these years?'

She made a quick involuntary step to meet him – then turned abruptly, he thought disdainfully, away. The next moment she had entered the house and Stephen Gallier was alone with his aching heart.

*   *   *

'Dr Gallier,' said Professor Starkie, inspecting his visitor, 'do you fully realise what you are proposing? Have you fully reflected on the consequences, if my theory should prove erroneous?'

Stephen Gallier nodded. 'I know the chances – and the dangers. And I offer myself for the experiment entirely foreseeing what danger may mean. At the worst it is only death.'

The professor paced the laboratory floor for a moment, then turned to Gallier with the light of enthusiasm in his eyes. 'You are a hero, Gallier, in a higher, nobler cause than ever fell to the lot of man . . .'

Gallier stopped him. 'Just tell me what is to be done.'

For answer, Professor Starkie unlocked a safe and took from it a small steel cylinder, such as is used by chemists for storing compressed gas. Holding it as though it were of priceless value, he confronted his visitor.

'I was a very young man when the possibility dawned on me that the ancient theory of the transmigration of souls might have a basis in solid fact. A lifetime of research scarcely took me a step closer towards proof. True, I was able to prove to myself that the soul was not so fast a prisoner within the body as scientists believe. By gradually weakening, debilitating the tissues, I found it possible to draw away from my physical self. I was able to stand for a brief period by the side of my own body – separate from it; but I was never

He threw the cylinder far out
into the dark shrubbery.

able to move from its vicinity.'

'But now you have met with success?'

'I am sure of it. I have isolated a gas which, when taken into the lungs, has a most remarkable action upon the whole body. Hitherto all my experiments have been upon animals, for a very good reason. The action, once initiated, cannot be arrested by any means I have been able to discover. The process is invariably the same. Once the gas is inhaled, all the bodily forces begin to subside. Slowly, but inevitably, the muscles lose their power of contraction; the tissues visibly collapse; the heart runs down until it is impossible to say from the pulse whether life exists or not. In fact, for hours before death actually takes place, the subject must be in exactly that state of debility, that extreme attenuation of bodily life, in which the soul is no longer fettered to the body, but is free at last to voyage abroad and seek some new living earthly tenement.'

'Tell me, would the man have the power to choose the living body into which his soul is to enter?'

'Dr Gallier, I know nothing – *nothing*. Yet why should it not be so? My belief is that there would be a fight for the citadel: then the strongest would win, and – *Stop!'*

Gallier had made a sudden movement towards the cylinder – but the professor held it from him. 'Man, are you mad? We must have no dead bodies accounted for! Dead men are stubborn facts, even in a hospital laboratory, and all the scientific explanations in the world would not save Professor Starkie FRS from the hangman. No, there is much to be thought of before the experiment can be commenced. Now listen to me!'

With smouldering impatience Gallier listened to the instructions. Ten minutes later he was in a hansom at the hospital gate, the fateful cylinder in his pocket, the professor's final warning ringing unheeded in his ears. Ten minutes later he was in his hotel room. He sat down at the table, wrote a short hurried note, and summoned a waiter: 'I am feeling extremely unwell. Take this letter as fast as you can to Dr Bute Walton in Grosvenor Crescent, and tell him to come as quickly as possible.'

Gallier waited until the door had closed, then, taking Professor Starkie's cylinder from his pocket, he turned the stop-cock gently on. The gas rushed screaming into the elastic store chamber. With trembling fingers Gallier set the mouthpiece to his lips, letting the sweet, faint current fill his lungs again and again. When it was quite exhausted he walked to the window and threw the cylinder far out into the dark shrubbery below. Then, already faint and giddy, he staggered towards his bed, and lay quietly down to await the coming of the man he envied of all others in the world.

* * *

Deep, blinding night, and a sense of falling, falling, through the limitless darkness. Then as swift an upward flight, meteor-like, through the black void again; far above into a world that seemed to be ringing with a thousand voices, and flashing with a thousand contending fires. Then down once more, yet slower now, and slower: until his feet seemed to touch firm ground; until the voices were lost in the distance; until all the lights were dwindled and gone, all save one that now burned steadily near him.

Conscious only of this one unchanging thing in the giddy swirl of his surroundings, Stephen Gallier fixed his eyes upon it, watching it until its familiar shape grew clear upon his mind. It was the flame of a candle. Slowly his vision cleared, his brain grew calmer. He saw that the light stood upon a table; that he himself was no longer prone upon his bed, but sitting by it. Looking down he became conscious of a startling change about his person. The clothes he wore were strange to him. He caught sight of his hands. White, strong, delicate – they could not be his! Yet he controlled them. He felt the weight of a gold watch in one; with the other he held fast to something – something that stretched out from the bedside. Cold, clammy – a dead hand!

With a cry, he threw it from him; staggered to his feet; turned, and chanced upon the mirror. Again a cry burst from his lips: he saw not his own blue eyes and sunburnt face and greying hair, but another face, one he had not seen for ten long years – Bute Walton's! He turned again to the bed: there on the quilt lay his own form, Stephen Gallier – shrunken to a shadow of its former strength, yet still plainly recognisable.

Shaking like an aspen, yet with a fierce joy already stirring within him, Gallier crossed to his suitcase. He drew out a brandy flask and drank deeply. The spirit ran through his veins like fire and lashed his fallen courage. He strode again to the mirror, again he looked at the dreadful thing upon the bed. The events of the foregoing hour came flooding back into his brain. The long wait as he lay upon the couch, his life ebbing away, his heart failing, the cold of death creeping up his limbs. Then the arrival of his former friend; his own soul's leap tiger-like upon him; the conflict as they seemed to fall grappling together through the outer darkness – he lived through it all once more.

And now the old drab lonesome life was ended, the barrier between him and the woman he worshipped was swept away. He was free to go to her now as swiftly as his feet could take him. Her love was his: his strong arms would soon be round her, his kisses thick as rain upon her lips.

For a moment Stephen Gallier stood, laughing softly with himself. Then he tugged at the bell-rope. 'You have called me too late,' he said when answer came to his summons. 'The gentleman is dead; how, it is impossible to say at present. Ask the manager to step up. And send word to the nearest police station.'

As in a dream he made the necessary dispositions: then at last he found himself outside in the dripping winter's night. Bute Walton's carriage was waiting, the coachman leaning from his box for instructions.

'Home!'

Home! The heart of Stephen Gallier was going home at last to the woman whose name had been seared upon it so many long years. Now she was his, his only, for all time!

At last the carriage drew out of the Piccadilly crush, and turned into the silent crescent. Gallier was out before the wheels had ceased to revolve.

'Is your mistress still up?'

The servant looked at his burning face with surprise, but stuttered that she had just gone to her room. Gallier hurried up the stairs. He had not dared to show his ignorance of the house. He must find his way unaided. Door after door he passed, listening intently outside one, softly opening another. Only darkness in this room – darkness and the rattle of sleet on the panes. In this one a dim rosy light with a supper table spread for two. Then at last a door close-curtained. He pulled the drapery gently aside, softly turned the handle. A bright glow of firelight within – and silence again. Silence? There was a sound there, suppressed but still audible – the sound of passionate weeping. Gallier saw a woman sitting by a table, her face buried in her arms, her shoulders heaving up and down with the grief that was racking her.

'Lettie!' What sorrow could be hers in this great luxurious house, with all that wealth and refinement could bring her?

Silently she stood, trying to bring a smile of welcome into her glance. But it was in vain: the tears flower more abundantly than ever. 'No, don't speak to me, Bute. Leave me alone for a little while. I – I –'

He had sprung forward, love, joy, infinite passion ringing in his voice, as he tried to comfort her. But at his first touch she rose again, beating him wildly off with both hands. 'No, Bute, I cannot bear it any longer. I cannot bear to hear your loving words: you so brave and kind and trusting. An end must soon come to all this wickedness and deceit: and why not now, why not tonight? Bute, I must speak – sooner or later you must know – O God in Heaven, help me to tell him!'

Her face buried in her hands, she went rapidly on. 'Bute, listen and judge me. I wronged you when I married you, for I loved another. Oh Bute, you cannot tell how hard I tried to overcome my love for him, but it has always mastered me. And now chance has brought us together again after so many years. Only last night I met him face to face. And now, Bute, I cannot eat your bread, and bear your kisses, knowing I love this man. You must let me go away, and live my life out in some distant hiding-place far away from this great temptation.'

Her words died away, whelmed in her pitiful sobbing. The man she thought to be her husband stood before her, white as death itself.

Stephen Gallier leaped upon the window-sill and hurled himself into the night.

As she ceased, his grip descended, fastening on her wrist like a vice. 'Tell me his name. Not –'

'Yes, Stephen Gallier.'

She was at his feet now, clasping them with both hands. Silently he drew away from her, away from the room. Blindly, not knowing whither his feet led him, he passed into the upper regions of the house. He felt himself choking. Air! Tottering to a window, he threw it open.

'There is no recall – none' – it had been the professor's last warning. But yesterday the thing he most coveted in all the world, this woman's love, was his and he did not know it. But he had meddled with Eternity, and the Great Machine had caught him up and annihilated him. Now love and life and honour, his very soul even, were lost to him.

The cloud rift closed above; a great darkness was suddenly upon everything. It was as if the ultimate Gate of Hope were even then shutting against him. With a last despairing cry, he leaped upon the window-sill, and hurled himself out into the night.

6 The last stand of the Decapods

**Some animals not recorded
in the natural history textbooks**

The Last Stand of the Decapods *(Frank T. Bullen, 1901)*

The Purple Terror *(Fred M. White, 1899)*

The Lizard *(Cutcliffe Hyne, 1898)*

'These animals lack only the single quality of size to make them all-powerful and all-desolating, and this quality they have not been able to attain owing to the lack of favouring conditions. How easily it might have been otherwise . . .'

This *Strand* contributor was indulging in one of man's favourite ways of teasing himself — to imagine that homo sapiens is not really the dominant species on earth. How easily it might be otherwise! At any moment some accident — a shift in climate, the sudden appearance of a particular nutrient conducive to growth — could upset the balance of nature. Natural selection, operating undisturbed in some remote part of the world where man's attention is not directed, could at this moment be producing a new race of super-ants, super-eagles, super-porpoises. Or locked beneath the Arctic ice, deep in mountain caves or under picturesque Scottish lochs, monstrous survivals of the past may be waiting to make a sensational come-back.

It wouldn't necessarily be such a bad thing, either. Some other species are much prettier, much gentler, much kinder than man: suppose they were much cleverer into the bargain! Such were the Houyhnhnms whom Lemuel Gulliver encountered on his fourth and final voyage — a friendly, gentle race who were horrified at their guest's account of humankind. He liked them so much better than his own kind that after he returned home it was years before he could endure the company — let alone the smell — of his fellow-creatures.

The barque 'British Banner' attacked by a sea serpent on 5th April 1860. Though not all sightings were as dramatic as this, there were many well-authenticated encounters with marine monsters throughout the nineteenth century.

Generally, however, when some freak of nature upsets the balance and some animal or insect finds itself suddenly superior to man, it is noteworthy that it is generally one of the nasty ones: only Wells, as always more imaginative than his colleagues, allows his Food of the Gods to be consumed by pussy cats and puppy dogs as well as by wasps and rats. And the species which are stumbled upon by explorers — survivals from the past, like those discovered by Conan Doyle's Professor Challenger in his *Lost World* — are neither pleasant to look at nor nice to know. Alas, there generally has to be a fight to the death then and there, with the unfortunate result that no real rapprochement between humanity and the strange creature is so much as attempted: this also means that no evidence is forthcoming to prove the tale, and the narrator usually has to conclude his tale by complaining that nobody will believe him. Professor Challenger was one of the few who were

GULLIVER AND THE HOUYHNHNMS Secure in his pre-eminence, man has often tried to fancy how it would be if some even more superior species were to appear on the scene. In Swift's last voyage, Gulliver meets the Houghnhms, wise horses who surpass humans not only in intelligence but also in moral virtue.

able to bring back documentary evidence, in the form of a pterodactyl which escapes and terrorises London before winging its way back to the past. But from what we see of it, it doesn't seem likely that it would have ever made much of a household pet.

This unfriendliness isn't necessarily caused by any special vindictiveness – rather, it's because that is the law of the jungle. Red in tooth and claw they've always been, red in tooth and claw they will stay! But in any case, who ever heard of a friendly giant spider, a friendly giant crab, a friendly giant lizard?

THE LAST STAND OF THE DECAPODS

by FRANK T. BULLEN

ELL was it for the whales that, living always near the sea, they had formed aquatic habits: for it was becoming clearer all the time that shore life would soon be too onerous for them. Vast dragon-like shapes, clad in complete armour that clanged as the wide-spreading bat-wings bore them swiftly through the air, were liable to descend upon them from the skies and with horrid rending by awful shear-shaped jaws, speedily strip from their bodies the masses of succulent flesh. And other enemies weird of shape and swift of motion, although confined to the earth, found the sluggish ponderous whale an easy prey.

But in the sea the whales' huge bulk was more a help than a hindrance. Gradually they grew to use the land less and less as they became more and more accustomed to the food provided in plenty by the inexhaustible ocean: continual practice enabled them to husband the supplies of air which they took in on the surface for use beneath the waves: their hind legs dwindled away and disappeared, their vast and far-reaching tails spread out laterally into flexible fans with which they could propel themselves through the waves at speeds to which their swiftest progress upon land had been but a snail's crawl: their fore-legs grew shorter and wider, until all that was left of these once ponderous supports were elegant fan-like flippers, steadying vanes to keep the whole great structure in its proper position.

121

But their invasion of the sea had a result entirely unforeseen by them. Gradually they found that, in order to satisfy the demands of their huge stomachs, they were fain to follow their prey into deeper and deeper waters, meeting as they went with other and stranger denizens of those mysterious depths. Until at last the sperm whale met that nightmare monstrosity that crouches in the darkling depths of ocean, hugest of all the mollusca, the kraken.

There in his native gloom, vast, formless, and insatiable, brooded the awful Thing. Spread like a living net whereof every mesh was armed, sensitive and lethal, this fantastic complication of horrors took toll of all the sea-folk, needing not to pursue its prey, needing only to lie still, devour, and grow. Sometimes moved by mysterious impulses one of these chimeras would rise to the sea-surface and bask in the beams of the offended sun, poisoning the surrounding air with its charnel-house odours, and occasionally finding within the clutching of its tentacles some specimens of the highest product of Creation, man himself. With a cylindrical body seventy feet in length, which it was nevertheless able to propel through the water at twenty miles per hour with the aid of an inky jet which, mingling with the encompassing sea, filled the neighbourhood with a gloom so deep that none save one of its own species could see either to fight or fly: with never-closing eyes whose pupils, fully two feet in diameter, enabled their possessor to discern what was going on amidst the thick darkness that itself had raised, so that while all other organisms were groping blindly in the gloom, it might work its will among them: and above all, armed not merely with the eight tentacles of the octopus, but with two additional arms, whose eighty-foot length was double that of the others – the eight studded with saucer-like hollows, each with a fringe of curving claws, capable of holding anything they touched by a suction so severe that it would strip flesh from bone while the cruel claws, large as those of a full-grown tiger, lacerated and tore the prey until the quivering victim yielded up its innermost secrets, and each gifted with an almost independent power of volition, bringing its prey inwards to where in the centre of all those infernal purveyors lay a black chasm whose edges were shaped like the upper and lower mandibles of a parrot, and these completed the work begun so well – the two outliers comparatively slender to within two feet or so of their ends, there expanding into broad paddle-like masses thickly studded with further sucking discs, forever searching the surrounding water with relentless menace . . . So built, so equipped, the kraken justifies the assertion that no imagination could add anything to the terror-breeding potentialities of its aspect.

And so on a momentous day a ravenous sperm whale, hunting eagerly for wherewithal to satisfy his craving, suddenly found himself encircled by many long, cable-like arms. They clung, they tore, they sucked. But whenever a stray end of them flung itself across the bristling parapet of the whale's lower jaw it was promptly bitten

The whale settled down seriously to the demolition of his prize.

122

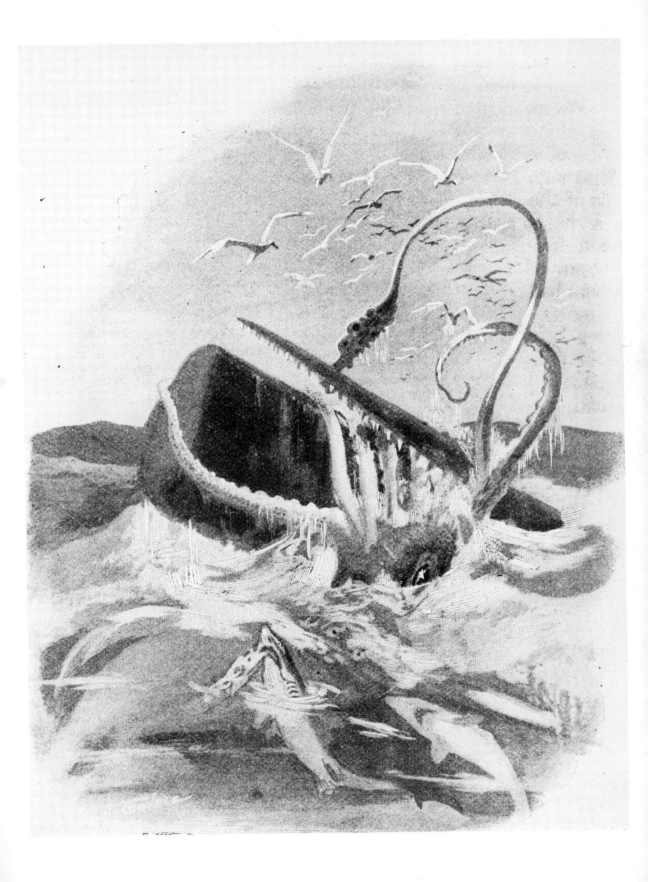

off, and, a portion having found its way down into the craving stomach of the big mammal, it was welcomed as good beyond all other food yet encountered. Now, what had originally been an accidental entrapping changed into a vigorous onslaught and banquet. The foul mass of the kraken found itself, contrary to all previous experience, being compelled to leave its infernal shades, and without any previous preparation for such a change of pressure to visit the upper air. The fact was that the whale, its stock of air exhausted, had put forth a supreme effort to rise, and found that although unable to free himself from those enormous cables he was actually competent to raise the whole mass. What an upheaval! Even the birds, allured in their thousands by the strong carrion scent, fled from that appalling vision, their wild screams of affright filling the air with lamentation. The tormented sea foamed and boiled. The whale, having renewed his store of air, settled down seriously to the demolition of his prize. Length after length of tentacle was torn away from the central crown and swallowed, gliding down the abysmal throat of the gratified mammal in snaky convolutions until he could contain no more.

The proportions of the kraken were so immense that, even when the whale had eaten his utmost, there remained sufficient for a dozen of his companions, had they been there. This was a momentous discovery indeed – a new source of supply that promised to be inexhaustible. So, in the manner common to his people, he wasted no time in convening a gathering of them as large as could be collected. Far over the glassy surface of that quiet sea lay gently rocking a multitude of vast black bodies. The epoch-making news circulated in perfect silence, for to them has from earliest times been known the secret that is only just beginning to glimmer upon the verge of human intelligence, the secret of thought-transference. And having learned of the treasures held for them by the deep waters, they separated and went upon their rejoicing way.

Then followed a time of feasting without parallel. Without any fear, the whales sought out and devoured one after another of these vast uglinesses. Occasionally some rash youngster, full of pride, would hurl himself into a smoky network of tentacles only to be trapped and perish miserably, his cable-like sinews falling slackly and his lungs suffused with crimson brine. But even then the advantage gained by the kraken was a barren one, for the bulk of his victim was too great, his body too firm in its build, for the victor to succeed in devouring his prize.

This desultory warfare was waged for long until, driven to a community of interest unknown before, the krakens sought one another out with an idea of combining against the new enemy. For, knowing their size and their power, they could not yet bring themselves to believe that they were to become the helpless prey of these newcomers. From the remotest recesses of ocean they came, that grisly gathering, their silent progress spreading unprecedented dismay among the fairer inhabitants of the sea. Only dimly can we imagine what must have been the appearance of those vast masses of writhing flesh, as through the palely gleaming phosphorescence of those depths they sped backwards in leaps of a hundred fathoms each, their terrible arms, close clustered together, streaming behind them like Medusa's hair magnified ten thousand times in size, and with each snaky tress bearing a thousand mouths instead of one.

The elder and mightier were full of disdain at the reports they were furnished with, utterly incredulous as to the ability of any created thing to injure them – for while no one in all their hosts was of lesser magnitude than sixty feet long, some, the acknowledged leaders, discovered themselves like islands, their carcasses huge as that of an ocean liner and their tentacles capable of overspreading an entire village.

Suddenly into the midst of their meeting came darting a messenger squid, bearing the news that a school of sperm whales numbering at least a thousand were coming at top-speed direct for their place of meeting. Instantly by one movement there uprose from the sea-bed so dense a cloud of sepia that for many miles round the clear bright blue of the ocean became turbid, stagnant and foul. The birds that hovered overhead took fright and fled with discordant shrieks in search of sweeter air and cleaner sea. But below the surface there was the silence of death.

Twenty miles away, under the bright sunshine, an advance guard of whales came rushing on. Line abreast, their bushy breath rising like the regular steam-jets from a row of engines, they dashed aside the welcoming wavelets, ravenous with hunger as well as full of fight. And after them the main body, spread over a space of thirty miles, came following on, the roar of their multitudinous march sounding like the roar of many waters.

Suddenly the advance guard, with stately elevation of the broad fans of their flukes, disappeared: by one impulse the main body followed. Down into the depths they bore until, with a thrill of joyful anticipation which set all their masses of muscle a-quiver, they recognised the scent of the prey. Without the faintest slackening of their rush they plunged forward into the abysmal gloom: down into that wilderness of waiting demons. And so, in darkness and silence like that of the beginning of things, battle was joined. Whale after whale succumbed, anchored to the bottom by such bewildering entanglements, such enlacements of tentacles that their vast strength was helpless to free them, their jaws bound hard together. But the decapods were in evil case. Massed as they were, they found themselves more often locked in unreleasable hold of their fellows than they did of their enemies. And the quick-shearing jaws of those foes shredded them into fragments, made nought of their bulk, revelled and frolicked among them exulting. Again and again the triumphant mammals drew off for air and from satiety, went and lolled upon the sleek oily surface in water now so thick that the fiercest hurricane that ever blew would have failed to raise a wave thereon.

So through a day and a night the slaying ceased not until those of the decapods left alive had disentangled themselves from their late associates and fled to depths and crannies where they fondly hoped their ravenous enemies could never come. Henceforth they were no longer lords of the sea: instead of being as hitherto devourers of all things living that crossed the radius of their outspread toils, they were now and for all time to be the prey of a nobler creation, a higher order of being, and at last they had taken their rightful position as creatures of usefulness in the vast economy of Creation.

THE PURPLE TERROR

by FRED M. WHITE

LIEUTENANT Scarlett's instructions were devoid of problems, physical or otherwise. To convey a letter from Captain Driver of the *Yankee Doodle,* in Porto Rico Bay, to Admiral Lake on the other side of the isthmus, was an apparently simple matter.

'All you have to do,' the captain remarked, 'is take three or four men in case of accidents. The aborigines are presumedly friendly.'

The aborigines aforesaid were Cuban insurgents. Little or no strife had taken place in the area, though it was known to be given over to the disaffected Cubans. True, the Spaniards and the Cubans alike were not exactly enamoured of the American flag, but Scarlett set off on his cross-country journey without expecting to encounter any obstacles more awkward than fifty miles of practically unexplored forest. For a West Point graduate with brains as well as smartness, it should not be too difficult a task.

A warrant officer, Tarrer by name, plus two A.B.'s of thews and sinews, along with a redoubtable mastiff, completed the party. By sunset on the first day they had covered six miles of their journey, and came to a village which pretended to be 'friends of the Americanos'. Scarlett doubted the fact, but the party made themselves tolerably comfortable in the village's only wine-shop, filled with Cubans who took absolutely no notice of the intruders. This might have been a sullen hostility – but an alternative reason was provided on the rude stage at the far end of the bar, whereon a girl was gyrating in a dance with a grace which caused the wreath of flowers around her shoulders to resemble a trembling zone of purple flame.

The dance over, the girl came forward, extending a shell prettily. As Scarlett smiled and dropped his quarter-dollar into the shell a coquettish gleam came into the velvety eyes. An ominous growl came from the lips of a bearded ruffian close by. But Scarlett was less interested in the girl than in the flowers which she had twined round her shoulder. An enthusiastic botanist, he knew enough to know they were orchids – and a kind unknown to collectors. The blooms were immensely large, of a deep pure purple with a blood-red centre.

'Tell me where you got them, pretty one,' he asked.

The bearded Cuban came closer. 'The señor had best leave the girl alone.'

'Though I certainly admire your good taste, it was the flowers which interested me.'

'The señor would like such blooms? It was I who brought them for Zara. I can show you where they grow.'

Every eye in the room was turned in Scarlett's direction. It seemed to him that a diabolical malice glistened on every dark face – save that of the girl, whose features paled. 'If the señor is wise, he will not . . .'

'Listen to the tales of a silly girl,' the man interrupted. 'Why, there is no harm where the flowers grow, if one is careful. I will be your guide for a gold dollar.'

Scarlett's scientific enthusiasm was aroused. It is not given to every man to present a new orchid to the horticultural world. 'We start at daybreak. Be ready.'

*　　　*　　　*

Tito was ready at daybreak. His insolent manner had disappeared. He was cheerful, alert, full of winning politeness. Only when Scarlett mentioned the orchid did a queer gleam flash through his eyes. A time was to come when Scarlett was to recall that look, but for the moment it was allowed to pass.

'The señor shall see the purple orchid, thousands of them. They have a bad name among our people, but that is nonsense. They grow in the high trees, and their blossoms cling to long green tendrils which are poisonous to the flesh. But the flowers are quite harmless, though we call them the devil's poppies.'

For hours they fought their way through the dense tangle. A heat lay over the land like a curse – a blistering, sweltering moist heat with no puff of wind. By sunset the party had had enough of it. They passed out of the underwood at length and approached a clump of huge forest trees on the brow of a ridge. All kinds of parasites hung from the branches; there were ropes and bands of green, and high up a fringe of purple glory.

'Surely that is the orchid?'

'A mere straggler,' Tito replied with a shrug, 'and out of our reach in any case. The señor will have all he wants and more tomorrow.'

'Yet it seems to me ...' Scarlett was beginning, and then he paused. For suddenly he saw among the branches a network of green cords like a spider's web, and in the centre of it, not a fly but a human skeleton! The arms and legs were stretched apart as if the victim had been crucified. The wrists and ankles were bound in the cruel web. Fragments of tattered clothing fluttered in the faint breath of the evening breeze.

Tito explained. 'Some plant-hunter, I think. He climbed into the tree and those green ropes twisted round his limbs as a swimmer is entangled in weeds. The more he struggled, the more the cords bound him. He would call in vain for help – and so he died.'

The explanation was plausible, but it by no means detracted from the horror of the discovery. The party pushed on in silence till they reached a clearing where Tito declared 'We will camp here, on this high ground. In the valley the miasma is dangerous.'

A torch was lit, and the party saw to their astonishment that the ground was littered with the skulls of animals – yes, and of human beings too: the skeletons of birds, beasts and men. A weird, shuddering sight. 'We can't possibly stay here!' Scarlett exclaimed.

Tito shrugged. 'There is nowhere else. Down in the valley there is the miasma. Further in the woods are snakes and jaguars. Bones are nothing.'

There was nothing for it but to make the best of it: but as they cleared a space for their camp, Scarlett noticed that the skeletons lay in a perfect circle, starting from the centre of the clump of trees arching above them. Tito suggested the religious rites of the natives as an explanation: Scarlett was unconvinced. 'There's something uncanny about this,' he told Tarrer, 'and I mean to get to the bottom of it.'

'As for me,' Tarrer yawned, 'I have but one ambition – my supper, followed by bed.'

*   *   *

Scarlett lay in the light of the fire, looking about him. He felt restless and uneasy. The air trembled to strange noises. There seemed to be something moving, writhing in the forest trees above his head. More than once it seemed to be a squirming knot of green snakes in motion.

Outside the circle, in a grotto of bones, Tito lay sleeping. A few moments before, his dark sleek head had been furtively raised, and his eyes seemed to gleam in the flickering firelight with malignant cunning. As he met Scarlett's glance he gave a deprecatory gesture and subsided.

'What the deuce does it mean?' Scarlett wondered. Was the Cuban jealous because the Americanos had paid his girl a little attention? Well, but what harm could he do them.

Nevertheless he determined to keep awake for a spell: and did so. Yet nothing occurred, though even the dog seemed to be conscious of some unseen danger, and whimpered in his dreams. Gradually Scarlett sank into sleep – only to be awakened by the dog howling in real earnest. He opened his eyes to see the mastiff snatched up by some invisible hand, carried far on high towards the branches of the trees, then flung down to earth with a crash. The big dog lay still as a log.

Nobody stirred, worn out with exhaustion. With teeth set and limbs that trembled, Scarlett crawled over to the dog.

The great black-muzzled creature was quite dead: the chest soaked with blood, the throat cut apparently with some jagged, saw-like instrument, away to the bone. Strangest of all, scattered all about the body were the great purple flowers of the orchid.

Scarlett felt his hair rising. He was frightened, more scared than he had been in his life before. But there must be some rational

The sleeping man was raised gently from the ground.

explanation for what had happened . . . Suddenly he saw falling a green bunch of cord which straightened into a long emerald line. It was triangular in shape, fine at the apex, and furnished with hooked spines. At regular intervals along it were the blossoms of the devil's poppy. For a time it dangled on the ground, apparently taking up moisture from the heavy dews of night. And then to his horror he saw the rope swing forward like a pendulum towards the shoulders of a sleeping seaman. Suddenly it became like the arm of an octopus. The line shook from end to end like the web of an angry spider when invaded by a wasp. It seemed to grip the sailor and tighten, and then, before Scarlett's affrighted eyes, the sleeping man was raised gently from the ground.

Now that a comrade was in danger Scarlett forgot his fear. He whipped his jack-knife from his pocket and slashed at the cruel cord. He half expected to meet with the stoutness of a steel strand, but to his surprise the feeler snapped like a carrot, bumping the sailor heavily on the ground.

He sat up, rubbing his eyes. 'That you, sir? What's the matter?'

'For the love of God, get up at once and help me to wake the others. We have come across the devil's workshop. All the horrors of the inferno are invented here.'

The bluejacket struggled to his feet. As he did so, the clothing from his waist downwards slipped about his feet, clean cut through by the teeth of the green parasite. All around his body, blood oozed from a ring of teeth marks.

'What does it mean, sir?' he screamed.

'Wake the others,' Scarlett shouted in reply.

Two or three more green tangles of rope came tumbling to the ground, straightening and quivering. The purple blossoms stood out like a frill on them. Like a madman Scarlett shouted, kicking his companions till they woke.

'I don't understand it at all,' Tarrer complained.

'Come out from under those trees, and I will explain.' But save for the wounded sailor, the party refused to believe his account – not even when he indicated the lifeless body of the dog.

By this time a dozen or more of the cords were hanging down in the darkness. Tarrer strode forward towards the trees. 'I'm going to investigate this for myself.'

'Come back, for God's sake!'

'Don't be ridiculous,' Tarrer smiled as he threaded his way between the slender emerald columns. And true enough, as they moved slowly and with a certain stately deliberation they seemed hardly likely to present any danger to a grown individual. Scarlett began to wonder if he had been dreaming after all.

But just then a whip-like trail of green touched Tarrer from behind, and in a lightning flash he was in the toils, bound with a terrible power.

'Cut me free!' he cried, 'I am being carried off my feet!'

ur knives were at work ripping
d slashing in all directions.

For a moment he seemed to be doomed, for every cord was converging in his direction. One after another, they twined themselves round him with sickening purpose.

Heedless of possible danger to himself, Scarlett darted forward, calling to his companions. Soon four knives were at work ripping and slashing in all directions. 'You two, keep your eyes open for fresh cords and cut them as they fall, instantly.'

131

The horrible green spines were round Tarrer's body like snakes. His face was white, his breath came painfully, for the pressure was terrible. It seemed to Scarlett to be one horrible dissolving view of green slimy cords and great weltering purple blossoms. The whole of the ground beneath their feet was strewn with them.

Tarrer had fallen forward half unconscious. He was supported now by but two cords above his head. The cruel pressure had been relieved. With one savage sweep of his knife Scarlett cut the last of the lines, and Tarrer fell like a log to the ground. A feeling of nausea, a yellow dizziness, came over Scarlett as he staggered beyond the dread circle. He saw Tarrer carried to a place of safety, and then the world seemed to wither and leave him in the dark.

*   *   *

'We ought to shoot the beggar!'

'I have a little plan of my own,' Scarlett replied, beckoning the Cuban over to them. 'It has come to my knowledge, you rascal, that you are playing traitor to us. Therefore we prefer to complete our journey alone.'

'The señor may do as he pleases. Give me my dollar and let me go.'

'We shall leave you here till we return. You will have plenty of food, you will be sheltered by the trees, and to make sure you remain here we shall tie you up to one of these trees for the next four-and-twenty hours.'

The insolence died out of the man's face, a cold dew came out over the ghastly green of his features. 'There is danger, señor, from snakes, and other things.'

'If this place was safe last night, it is safe today.'

Tito fell forward on his knees, howling for mercy, till Scarlett fairly kicked him up again. 'Make a clean breast of it, then.'

And so the story came out. Tito wanted to get rid of the Americanos. Would Cuba be any better off under the Americanos? By no means. Therefore it was the duty of every good Cuban to destroy the Americanos wherever possible. And so, knowing the habits of the purple orchid, he had bethought him of this means of destroying the Americanos – and assuaging his own jealousy at the same time.

'I'm not sure which I like the least,' Scarlett said to Tarrer, 'our friend here, or his purple orchid.'

'At least the flower has its good looks in its favour,' Tarrer suggested.

'I'm not so sure,' Scarlett replied, surveying the luxuriant blooms scattered at their feet. 'Somehow, after last night, I don't find them as beautiful as they were round the neck of that dancer.'

by CUTCLIFFE HYNE

IT is not expected that the general public will believe the statements which will be made in this paper. They are written to catch the eye of Mr Wilfred Cording (or Cordy) if he still lives, or of his friends and relations. Further details may be had from me (by any of these interested people) at Poste Restante, Wharfedale, Yorkshire. My name is Chesney, and I am sufficiently well known there for letters to be forwarded.

The matters in question happened two years ago on the last day of August. I had a small high-ground shoot near Kettlewell, but that morning dense mist made shooting out of the question. However, I wasn't sorry for an off-day, as there was a newly-found cave in the neighbourhood which I was anxious to explore – cave-hunting being, after shooting, my main amusement.

I suggested to my keeper that he should come with me to inspect the cave: he made some sort of excuse and I did not press the matter further. The dalesmen up there look on the local caves with more awe than respect. They will not own up to believing in bogles, but I fancy their creed runs that way. I had taken unwilling helpers cave-hunting with me before, and found them such a nuisance that I didn't press for the keeper's society. So I took candles, matches in a bottle, some magnesium wire, a small coil of rope, and a large flask of whisky, and set off alone.

I hadn't seen the cave for a week or more, and I was a good deal annoyed to find by the bootmarks that quite a lot of people had visited it in the interval. However, I hoped that the larger part were made by shepherds, and trusted that I might find the interior still untampered with.

The cave was easy enough to enter. There was a funnel-shaped slide of peat-earth and mud and clay to start with, well pitted with boot marks; and then there was a tumbled wall of boulders, slanting inwards, down which I crawled face uppermost till the light behind me dwindled. The way was getting pretty murky, so I lit up a candle to avoid accidents, stepped knee-deep into a lively stream of water, and went briskly ahead. It was an ordinary enough limestone cave so far, with inferior stalactites, and a good deal of wet everywhere. It did not appear to have been disturbed, and I stepped along cheerfully.

Presently I got a bit of a shock. The roof above began to droop downwards, slowly but relentlessly. It seemed as though my way was soon going to be blocked. However, the water beneath deepened, and so I waded along as far as possible. It was a cold job, the water was up to my chin, and the air was none of the best. I was beginning to think I had got wet through for no adequate result.

But there is no accounting for the freaks of caves. Just when I fancied I was at the end of my tether, I was able to stand erect once more: a dozen yards further on I came out onto dry rock, and was able to have a rest and a drop of whisky. The roof had quite disappeared to candlelight overhead, so I burned a foot of magnesium wire for a better inspection. It was really a magnificent cave, well furnished with stalactites above and stalagmites below: the candle burned brightly, showing me that the air was healthy enough. And yet the air in this cave did not altogether pass muster: there was something new about it, and anything new in cave smells is always suspicious. It wasn't the smell of peat, or iron, or sandstone, or fungus: it was a faint musky smell, rather sickly. When I inhaled a deeper breath of it, it came very near to making my flesh creep.

Before me stretched a tarn of black water, with a beach of white tumbled limestone on the far side. I pitched a stone into the water, shattering the surface for the first time in a million years. Yes, it's worth doing even a year of cave-hunting to do a thing like that. The stone sank with a luscious plop. The water was clearly very deep. But I was wet to the neck already, and didn't mind a swim. So with a lump of clay I stuck one candle in my cap, set up a couple more on the dry rock as a lighthouse to guide my return, lowered myself into the black water, and struck out. The smell of musk oppressed me, and I fancied it was growing stronger. So I didn't dawdle. Roughly, I guessed the pool to be some five-and-thirty yards across.

I landed amongst the broken limestone with a shiver and a scramble: the smell of musk was strong enough now to make me cough. But when I had stood up, and got the candle into my hand again, a thrill came through me as I thought I guessed the cause. A dozen yards further on was a broken cast where some monstrous uncouth animal had been entombed in the forgotten ages of the past, and mouldered away and left only the outer shell of its form and shape. For ages this, too, had endured; indeed, it had been violated only by the eroding touch of the water and some earth tremor within the last few days. A workman with plaster of Paris could have made an exact model of this beast which had been lost to the world's knowledge for so many weary millions of years.

It had been some sort of lizard or crocodile, and in fancy I was beginning to picture its restored shape in the National Museum, when my eye fell on something amongst the rubble which brought me to earth with a jar. I stopped and picked it up. It was a common white-handled penknife, of the variety sold by stationers for a shilling. On one side of it was the name of Wilfred Cording (or Cordy) scratched apparently with a nail. The work was neat enough to start with, but the engraver had wearied with his job, till the surname was too scratchy to be certain about.

On the hot impulse of the moment I threw the knife far from me into the black water, and swore. It is more than a little unpleasant for an explorer to find he has been forestalled. But since then I have more than once regretted the hard things I said against Cording (if that is his name). If the man is alive, I apologise to him. If, as I strongly suspect, he came to a horrible end in that cave, I tender my regrets to his relatives.

I looked upon the cast of the saurian now with the warmth of discovery quite gone. I was conscious of cold, and the musky smell was growing more and more unpleasant. I think I should straightaway have gone back to daylight and a change of clothes if I hadn't thought I could see the outline of another cast. It was hazy, as a thing of the kind would be if seen through the medium of sparsely transparent limestone, and by the light of a solitary paraffin wax candle. I kicked at it petulantly.

Some flakes of stone shelled off, and I distinctly heard a more extensive crack. I kicked harder – with all my might, in fact. More flakes shelled away, and there was a little volley of cracks. It did not feel like kicking against stone. It was like kicking against something that gave. And I could have sworn that the musky smell increased. I felt a curious glow coming over me that was part fright, part excitement, part nausea; but plucked up my courage and kicked again and again. The limestone flew up in tinkling showers. There was no doubt now about there being something springy underneath, and that it was the dead carcass of another lizard I hadn't doubt. Here was luck, here was a find. Here was I the discoverer of the body of a prehistoric beast, preserved in the limestone down through all the ages just as mammoths have been preserved in Siberian ice. As I kicked and battered at the harsh scaly skin of this anachronism, which ought to have perished body and bones ten million years ago, I wondered whether they would make me a baronet for the discovery.

Then of a sudden I got a start. I could have sworn the dead flesh moved beneath me.

But I shouted aloud at myself in contempt. Ten million years: it was impossible. And then I got a further start, a more solid one. While I was raising a boulder for a further blow, a splinter of stone broke away as if pressed up from below, flipped up in the air. My blood chilled, and for a moment the loneliness of that unknown cave oppressed me. But I told myself that I was an old hand: that this was childishness. I continued my battering until a further movement left me in no possible doubt – the beast was actually stirring of its own accord.

Stirring – and alive. It was writhing and straining to leave the rocky bed where it had lain quiet through all those countless cycles of time, and I watched it in a very petrifaction of terror. Its efforts threw up whole basketfuls of splintered stone at a time. I could see the muscles of its back ripple at each effort. I could see the exposed part of its body grow in size every time it wrenched at the walls of that semi-eternal prison.

Then, as I looked, it doubled up its back like a bucking horse, and drew out its stumpy head and long feelers, giving out the while a thin small scream like a hurt child: and then with another effort it pulled out its long tail and stood upon the debris of the limestone, panting with a new-found life.

I gazed upon it with a sickly fascination. Its body was about the bigness of two horses. Its head was curiously short, but the mouth opened back almost to the forearm; and sprouting from the nose were two enormous feelers, each at least 6 ft. long, tipped with fleshy tendrils like fingers which opened and shut tremulously. In colour it was a bright grass-green. And worst of all was the musky smell.

All this while I had stood motionless, but the beast must have heard some slight movement. I could not see any ears, but it heard me, no doubt of that. Worse, it hobbled round clumsily with its jointless legs, and waved its feelers in my direction. I could not make out any eyes: its sensitiveness seemed to lie in those fathom-long feelers and in the fleshy fingers which twitched at the end of them.

Then it opened its great jaws and yawned cavernously, and came towards me. It seemed to have no trace of fear of hesitation. It hobbled clumsily on, exhibiting its monstrous deformity in every movement, and preceded always by those hateful feelers.

For a while I stayed in my place, too paralysed with horror at this awful thing I had dragged up from the forgotten dead. But then one of its feelers touched me, and the fleshy fingers pawed my face. I leaped into movement again. The beast was hungry after its fast of ten million years . . . I turned and ran.

It followed me. In the feeble light of the one solitary candle I could see it hobbling – and hobbling faster and less clumsily now as it worked the rust of ages out of its cankered joints. Presently it was following me with a speed equal to my own.

If the huge beast had shown anger, eagerness, any feelings, it would have been less horrible: but it was absolutely unemotional in

I turned and ran.

its hunt, and this in turn came near to making me feel that I was lost, that I should surrender myself to the inevitable. I wondered dully whether there had been another beast entombed beside it, and whether that had eaten up the man who owned the penknife.

But that thought suggested an idea to me. I had a stout knife in my own pocket, and I drew it out and turned to defend myself just as the feelers with their fringe of fumbling fingers were agonisingly close to me. I slashed at them viciously, and felt my knife grate against their armour. I might as well have hacked at an iron rail.

Still, the attempt did me good. There is an animal love of fighting stowed away in the bottom of us all somewhere, and mine woke then. I don't know that I expected to win: but I did intend to do the largest possible amount of damage before I was caught. I made a rush, stepped with one foot on the beast's creeping back, and leaped astern of him: the beast gave its thin small whistling scream, and turned quickly in chase.

We doubled, turned, sprawled, leapt among the slimy boulders: and every time we came to close quarters I stabbbed with my knife, though without ever finding a joint in its armour. It was clear that this could not go on. The beast grew in strength and activity, and probably in dumb anger though it gave no sign of it; but I meanwhile was growing more blown, more bruised, more exhausted every moment.

At last I tripped and fell. The beast with its clumsy waddle shot past me before it could pull up, and in desperation I threw one arm up to drive the knife with the full force of my body into the underneath part of its body.

That woke it at last. It writhed, and it plunged, and it bucked with a frenzy that I had never seen before, and its scream grew in piercingness till it was as strong as the whistle of a steam engine. Again and again I planted my vicious blows, until it shook itself free in desperation and set off at its hobbling gait directly for the water. It plunged in, swam briskly with its tail, then I saw it dive and disappear for good.

And what next? I took to the water too, and swam as I had never swum before. It was that or nothing – risk the swim, or stay and be eaten. How I got across I do not know. How I landed I do not know. How I got down the windings of that cave is more than I can say, and whether the beast followed me I do not know either. Somehow I got to daylight again, staggering like a drunken man. I struggled as far as the village, noting how the people ran from me. At the inn the landlord cried out as though I had been the plague. It seemed that the musky smell I had brought with me was unendurable, though by this time the mere detail of a smell was far beneath my notice. But I was stripped from my stinking clothes, and washed, and put to bed, and a doctor came and gave me an opiate; and when twelve hours later wakefulness came to me again, I had the sense to hold my tongue. All the village wanted to know where the smell came from: I said I must have fallen into something.

And there the matter ends for the moment. I go no more cavehunting, and I offer no help to those who do. But if the man who owns that white-handled penknife is alive, I should like to compare experiences with him.

7 The last days of Earth

Extra-terrestial adventures

Our Second Voyage to Mars *(Anonymous, 1887–90)*

The Last Days of Earth *(George C. Wallis, 1901)*

When you haven't yet solved the problem of controlled flight off the surface of your own planet, it's a little premature to start planning visits to anyone else's. Today interplanetary travel is the archetype of science fiction, but we can hardly blame the writer of 1900 if his imagination seldom penetrated beyond the earth's atmosphere. The wonder is that any of them did so.

The possibility of life existing in other worlds had already been aired and debated, but the astronomer Sir Robert Ball pooh-poohed all suggestions for trying to communicate with Mars. It took the great imaginers — Verne and Wells — to tackle the problem of more direct contact with the rest of the universe.

Both despatched expeditions to the moon. Verne stuck to well-tried methods, exploiting the technology of heavy artillery to project his rocket, and at the same time bombarding his reader with impressive salvoes of figures to prove his case. Wells, more cunning, and at the same time more progressive in his thinking, has his hero discover an anti-gravitational substance which neatly sidesteps the problem.

For at this stage, the problems were basically mechanical ones — how to get there, what to do when you do get there, and ultimately, how to get home again. Verne, entirely absorbed in his practical nuts and bolts, produces chapter and verse for every stage of his lunar voyage, carrying us along with him every inch of the way — who are we to argue?

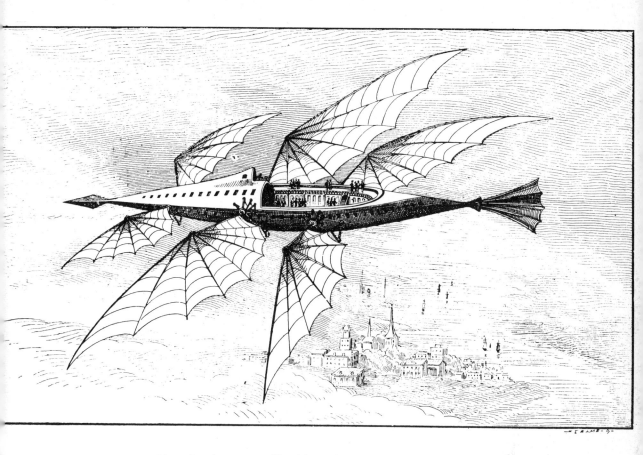

son, generally the most
ctical of inventors, seems
ely to have stayed clear of
g machines for the most
. The 'Daily Graphic', which
ted this impressive project,
quiet as to the technological
ects of the device, but it
ld appear that Edison
saged a system of
hanically flapping wings for
ulsion as well as lift.

markable prediction of a
eship shedding its capsule,
scene from Le Faure's 'Les
insons Lunaires' of 1893
ears astonishingly prophetic
gh in fact the technical
getry of the book is naive in
extreme.

Verne's characters, like himself, are completely preoccupied with the mechanical aspect of their enterprise: they have no time for more than the most cursory doubts, hesitations or anxieties. Bedford and Cavor, the members of Wells' expeditionary force, are a little more human: but even they have no time to spare for the psychological overshadowings which complicate the lives of the space voyagers of later decades, when physical problems have been solved only to be replaced by questions of emotional adjustment, nervous unbalance, ethical doubt.

Psychology apart, however, all the basic conventions of modern space fiction had been established by 1900 or so. What sort of reception should you expect when landing on another world? The Selenites discovered by Wells' team furnished the pattern for the bug-eyed monsters with which tradition has subsequently made us familiar — so familiar that we would be positively disconcerted if any other type of being descended from a flying saucer. Would they be friendly? Then as now, extra-terrestrial beings were apt to be suspicious and resentful: what's more, they would be more intelligent than ourselves — though fortunately, not *too* intelligent. We must not expect to be able to outwit them — but with luck we should be able to beat a successful retreat back to our space-craft and somehow return to the snug security of planet Earth.

OUR SECOND VOYAGE TO MARS

ANONYMOUS

UST as, among you on Earth, a few adventurous tourists annually go to see the land of the Midnight Sun – Norway – so here on Venus we think it pleasant and desirable for every one occasionally to spend a summer in the Arctic regions, and to stay, a few days at least, at the Pole itself. Perhaps the time may come when this will be the case on Earth, but vast progress in command over nature will be required before men can even reach the Poles. I expect it can only be done by perfecting the art of flight, or aeronautics, for the only convenient way of reaching the North or South Pole of either Venus or Earth is by flight.

We descended amid the great ring chain of mountains, peaks of heights of ten to twenty miles, compared to which your Mount Everest and Mont Blanc would be but hills. Even coming from the wonderful and awful realms of eternal light, the sight of the cascades pouring from the glaciers in the summer thaw was most beautiful. We poised our car over the glittering domes and towers of the great City of the North Pole: then slowly descended amid the plaudits of the crowds gathered to welcome us home.

As we alighted we were welcomed by the thousands of visitors at the Polar city. Joyous was our welcome, and deep our gratitude to Divine Providence, as we descended from the car which had borne us so well through the dangers of our awful, yet glorious, solar journey. We now noticed how it was encrusted with many metals which had fallen on it in the form of metallic rain as we had got near the Sun-spot, and now were crystallised round it in a strange form of metallic efflorescence. Tiny cubes of copper, iron, magnesium, cobalt were there. The record of our near approach to the Sun was on the car itself.

A congress was summoned, the third day after our arrival, to hear what we would relate of our journey. We told all we had seen, and showed the specimens we had collected from Mercury and the solar regions. Ezariel, the chief speaker of our party, proposed that now, since we had as mere voyagers visited the worlds around us, a more thorough exploration of one or two worlds would be desirable. The two that especially suggested themselves were Mars and the Earth.

poised our car over the
ering domes and towers of
great city of the North Pole.

Axorian, Prince of the City of the North Pole, urged that there would be a danger of our being observed and detected: but Ezariel parried this difficulty by proposing that our party should confine itself to going around the two planets and photographing carefully all the scenery of each, and to land in some remote part of Mars, and on the Earth to rest in the wilds of Central Australia and perhaps in Equatorial Africa, where we could examine the vegetable and animal life without risk of discovery.

This view was accepted by the congress. The great nature-subduer, Ornalion, was entrusted with the construction of a large car for twenty specialists to go through space to Mars and the Earth, to examine in each world the wondrous works of the great Creator. It was provided with powerful magnets and anti-gravitating machinery, and was of the strongest materials. In it a large quantity of specimens, and also all requisite apparatus, could be stored. In less than a quarter of one of our years I was once more flying through infinite space to the regions of the ruddy world of Mars.

The spot we chose to rest on was Hall's Snow Island, as an unfrequented and desolate region, yet not far from the great centres of Martian life. Here we landed by night and divided into two parties. The larger party set off upon an aerial expedition around Mars, and, poised in mid-air at great heights above the atmosphere, photographed the divers scenes of the planet, so recording all that was to be observed for the philosophers and museums of our world. In the meantime Ulnorion was to accompany me on or near the surface of the planet, disguised, as nearly as we could, in the Martian costume and aspect, which in truth was very difficult on account of our smaller size.

According to this plan we flew across to the Lagrange peninsula, and thence into the interior of Secchi Continent. Here the great system of canals struck our attention. They looked artificial, yet in width were like sounds or straits, but stretched for hundreds of miles, as clear from any undulation as if they had been drawn with a ruler. On their surfaces were floating islands, crowded with houses and factories and towers, like moving cities. On their shores were also vast edifices, where we could see the great machines of the Martians working and moving. Like a huge spider's web they spread over the crimson expanse of land.

We resolved to go to where my former Martian guide lived, that by his aid we might obtain more information about this gorgeous world. I found without difficulty his home – a domed house with metal ornaments beneath the ruddy foliage of the forest. I led Ulnorion to the door and then, noticing one of the windows open, I signed to him to fly in after me. My old friend was there, and was was much alarmed at first at the unexpected apparition of two beings from another world, for I had cast off my disguise so that he might know me. But then recovering himself, he recognised me as his former friend and guest. He welcomed us with the Martian rites of

greeting, and lighted the sacred fire upon the pillar, and offered us warm food. Ulnorion was timid and ill-at-ease: there is a natural shrinking of all creatures from beings of another world, and Ulnorion and our Martian host shrank from each other instinctively. But as time went on this lessened.

I suggested to Ulnorion that he might ask any questions he wished about the ruddy world in which we were. As I expected, his first question was about the wonderful canals. 'Will you explain,' he asked through me as his interpreter, 'these huge canals which mark several of your continents? They do not seem natural, more like vast engineering works.'

'They are mainly artificial works, though utilising our rivers and lakes. Our command over natural forces has in recent times become very great. So we resolved, for our own convenience, to turn the rivers and lakes into great canals. Water and land combined produce food: left to themselves we should not be able to produce the food we need to support so much life: thanks to the canals, we can do so. Again, on the water we can travel with rapidity and comfort from one part of our world to the other. Since we have had no wars we have been able to devote our force to the arts of peace.'

'What are those huge floating islands I saw on the canals?' asked Ulnorion.

'They are the floating cities. Instead of staying in one place, it is more convenient to move about. Thus we can live in a perpetual summer, and not merely leave our homes, but take our houses and gardens with us over the waters from land to land, drawing food both from land and water.' And he went on to explain how the oceans of Mars provide an inexhaustible store of food, with the huge store of edible molluscs (somewhat like your oysters) which fill them. Even on Earth the supply of food by the ocean would be inexhaustible: and perhaps in ages to come, when every land is over-populated, man may be forced as the Martians to establish fish-farms in shallow artificial seas to supplement the food supply.

'There is much in what you say,' I replied. 'If Northern Africa or Australia had some such system of canals as this, they would produce much more and suffer less from drought and desert.'

We issued forth from the house, and mounting on a hill close by, watched the Sun slowly descend over the crimson plain and the vast green network of canals which stretched in all directions at our feet. We conversed until the shadows of evening gathered in, then watched while the dying rays of the Sun shone on the ruddy forest-glades, slowly giving place to the two bright evening stars – Earth with her little satellite the Moon, and Venus our own bright home.

THE LAST DAYS OF EARTH

by GEORGE C. WALLIS

 MAN and a woman sat facing each other across a table in a large room. They were talking slowly, and eating – eating their last meal on earth. The end was near; the sun had ceased to warm, was but a red-hot cinder outwardly; and these two, to the best of their belief, were the last people left alive in a world-wilderness of ice and snow and unbearable cold.

As they talked, their fingers were busy with a row of small white knobs let into the surface of the table, and marked with various signs. At the pressure of each knob a flap in the middle of the table opened, and a small glass vessel, with a dark semi-liquid compound steaming in it, was pushed up. As these came, in obedience to the tapping of their fingers, the two ate their contents with tiny spoons. There was no other dining apparatus or dinner furniture.

The meal over, a silence fell between them. The man did not look at his fair companion, but beyond her, at a complicated structure projecting from the wall. This was the Time Indicator, whose symbols told him that it was just a quarter to thirteen in the afternoon of Thursday, July 18th, 13,000,085 A.D. He reflected that the long association of the place with time-recording had been labour spent in vain. The room stood on the site of the ancient Greenwich, named by its now dead and cold inhabitants Grenijia.

From the Indicator, the man's gaze went round the room. He noted the things that were so familiar to him – the severely plain walls, transparent on one side, but without window-frame or door: the chilling prospect of a faintly-lit expanse of snow outside: the big telescope: the electric radiators that heated the place, forming an almost unbroken dado round the walls: the globe of pale brilliance that hung in the middle of the room and assisted the twilight glimmer of the day: the neat library of books and photo-phono cylinders and the tier of speaking machines: the bed in the further corner, surrounded by more radiators: the two ventilating valves: the dull disc of the Pictorial Telegraph: the thermometer let into a vacant space of floor. On this last his glance rested.

'A whole degree, Celia, since yesterday. And the dynamos are giving out current at a pressure of 6000 volts. Any further fall of temperature will close the drama of this planet. Shall we go tonight?'

There was no fear or resentment in his voice, nor in the voice that answered him. Long ages of mental evolution had weeded out all the petty vices and unreasoning passions from the mind of man.

'I am ready at any time, Alwyn. I do not like to go; I do not like the risk of going; but it is our duty to the humanity behind us.'

'Your eyelashes are damp, Celia. You are not crying? That is too archaic.'

'I must plead guilty. We are not yet so thoroughly adjusted to our surroundings as to be able to crush down every weak impulse. But I will not give way again. Shall we start at once?'

'I had thought of taking a last look round the world – we have three hours' daylight yet.'

Celia sat beside him on the couch facing the disc of the Pictorial Telegraph. His left hand clasped her right: both were cold. With his right hand he held down a lever, one of many. The side wall became opaque; the globe above ceased to be luminous. A moving scene grew out of the dullness of the disc: a telegraphically-transmitted view of the place which had once been Santiago, Chile. There were the ruins of an immense white city there now: while below it, below the marks of six successive beach-lines, a cold sea moaned over an icy bar and dashed in semi-frozen spray under the bluff of an overhanging glacier's edge. Out to sea great bergs drifted slowly.

There was no sign of life, neither of man nor beast, nor bird nor fish. Polar bears and Arctic foxes, blubber-eating savages and hardy seals, had long since passed away even from the tropic zone.

Another lever – and the Rock of Gibraltar appeared, rising from the ice-arched waters of a shallow strait, with a glacial vista stretching behind into the hazy distance – a vista of such intolerable whiteness that the watchers put on green spectacles to look at it. On the flat top of the Rock, which ages ago had been levelled to make it an alighting station for the Continental aerial machines, rose, gaunt and frost-encrusted, the skeleton framework of one of the last flying conveyances used by man.

Another lever, and Colombo glared lifeless on the disc. Another, and Nagasaki frowned over a black ice-filling sea. Yet more levers, and yet more scenes: everywhere ice and snow, and shallow slowly-freezing seas: countries black and plantless or covered with glaciers from the crumbling hills. No sign of life save the vestiges of man's long fight with the relentless cold – the ruins of his Cities of Heat: moats excavated to retard the glaciers: canals to connect the warmer seas: the skeletons of floating palaces: and in every daylight scene, the pale ghost of a dim red sun.

'It appears just as we have seen it these last two years,' said the the man, 'yet today the tragedy of it appals me as it has never done before. I feel tempted to do as our parents did – to seek the safety of the Ultimate Silence.'

'Not that, Alwyn – not that. From generation to generation this day has been foreseen and prepared for, and we promised, after we were chosen to remain, that we would not die until all the devices of our science failed. Let us get ready to leave at once.'

'I only said "tempted", Celia. Were I alone, I do not think I should break my word. And I am also curious. And you are here. Let me kiss you, Celia. That, at least, is not archaic.'

They walked hand-in-hand to a square space marked out on the floor, and one of them pressed a button on the wall. The square sank with them, lowering them into a dimmer room where the ceaseless hum of the dynamos became a throbbing roar. They saw, with eyes long used to faint light, the four great alternators spinning round the armatures; felt the fanning of the rapid revolutions on their faces. By the side of each machine they saw the queer-shaped chemical engines that drove them. Coal had long since been exhausted, along with peat and wood and all inflammable oils and gases; no turbines could work from frozen seas, no air wheels revolve in an atmosphere but slightly stirred by a faded sun. The power in chemical actions and re-actions, in transmutations and compoundings of the elements, was the last great source of power left to man in the latter days.

After a brief glance round the room, they pressed another button, and the lift went down to a still lower floor. Here a small lamp was turned on, and they stood before a sphere of bright red metal that filled the greater part of the room. They had not seen this many times in their lives. Its meaning was too forcible a reminder of a prevision for the time that had at last arrived.

The Red Sphere was made of a manufactured element, unknown except within the last million years, and so costly and troublesome to produce that only two had ever been built. It had been made 500 years before, for the purpose of affording the chosen survivors of humanity a means of escaping from the earth. For generations the Red Sphere and all appertaining to it had been mentioned with awe.

'Are you sure that it will carry us safely? – that you can follow out the Instructions?'

'The Instructions are simple. The necessary apparatus, and the ten years' supply of imperishable nutriment, are already inside. We have only to subject the Red Metal to our 6000 volt current for an hour, get inside, screw up the inlet, and cut ourselves adrift. The Red Metal, when electrified, becomes repulsive to gravitation and will so continue for a year and a half. By that time, as we shall travel at twice the speed of light, we should be more than halfway to one of the nearer stars, and so become subject to its gravitation. With the earth in its present position, we should make F.188, mag.2 of the 3rd order of spectra. Our sun belonged to the same order, and we know it has at least two planets.'

'But if we fall right into it, instead of just missing it? Or if we miss, but so closely as to be fused by its heat? Or miss it too widely and are thrown back into space on a parabolic or hyperbolic orbit? Or suppose we manage the happy medium, only to find there is no life or even chance of life upon the planets of that system? Or if there be life, but life hostile to us?'

'Those are the risks we have to take, Celia. And if necessary – well, there is enough fulminate of sterarium in the Sphere to shiver it and us to fine dust in the thousandth part of a second – if we wish. We shall always have that resource. Now I'll attach the dynamo leads to the Sphere. Get your little items of personal property together, and we shall be ready.'

Celia went up the lift again: Alwyn, after fixing the connections to the Sphere, switched the electric current into the framework of the vehicle. All the radiators in the Heat-House ceased to glow and all the lights went out, leaving them in absolute darkness and intense cold. They sat huddled together against the wall where they could feel the thrill of the humming dynamos. They could find few words to speak, but their thoughts were the busier. They looked back across the long fight of Man against the cold: how, even though armed with powers that to their ancestors would have made them seem as gods, men had retreated continually. They had migrated to other planets, only to find that there too the dying sun had made all life a fore-known lost battle. And now at last the days of Man on Earth were ended. The Time Indicator in the uppermost room rang the peal of the completed hour, and they knew that in

their own lives they must act the final scene in the long life-tragedy of earth.

In silence Alwyn handed Celia into the sphere – which shone a deeper red now and coruscated strangely in the light – and then followed her, drawing the screw section in after him and making it secure. Within, the Sphere was spacious and comfortable, and, save where thickly padded, transparent. It was also pleasantly warm, for the Red Metal was impervious to heat. The man's hand went to the lever that worked through the shell, and pushed aside the strong jaws of the spring clamp that held the Sphere down; and as it went, he looked into the woman's eyes.

There was a sudden shock that threw them staggering against each other for a moment; a rending, tearing, rolling crash of masonry and metal, and the Red Sphere rose through the falling ruins of the Heat-House and soared up into the night. One brief glimpse they had of the dials of the Time Indicator falling across a gap of the ruin; and then their eyes were busy with the white face of earth beneath and the clear brilliance of the starry dome above. And then the man and woman who had been chosen knew that they were alone in Space, bound they knew not whither.

yn's hand touched a tiny
ton that was embedded in the
ding.

8 What's to come is still unsure

Some predictions about the future of the world – and its end

In 1900, as we began by saying, everything suddenly became possible. But the scientist was not always the first to realise it. From time to time he would poke his head through his laboratory door and utter a 'Eureka!' – but it was a 'Eureka' so cautious, so hesitantly hedged about with ifs and buts, that it's a wonder anyone heard it at all.

It was the journalist who heard him, squatting outside the scientist's door, ears pricked for the faintest hint of a discovery. It was the journalist who was certain that if science *could*, then science *would*. True, it might take time: true, it might take money. But American industry had shown that where demand existed, supply could somehow be achieved at an economic price. And there was no doubt that demand existed for anything that the scientist might come up with.

So up the staircase which the scientist took so painstakingly, testing each step before trusting his weight to it, the journalist bounded lightly and exuberantly. Eureka – men would talk from one side of the globe to the other. Eureka – pictures would be transmitted across the ether. Eureka – men would fly like birds. Eureka – men would visit other planets. What was fiction in 1900 would be translated into fact by the century to come.

The pessimistic scientist

But even the journalist needs a skeleton of fact on which to drape his fiction: so the editor would send his reporters to beard the scientists in their dens. At this period, the den was generally a study lined with books – the current image which never sees the scientist except in a white coat, surrounded by tubes which fume and gurgle, was still to come. The scientist, deeply ensconced in a leather armchair, would be asked to make some predictions about the future.

THE END OF THE WORLD
Prophets of doom have pictured the world ending in any number of ways. In Flammarion's 'La Fin du Monde', of 1894, the Earth is consumed by a star which gradually approaches, though by the time it was as near as this illustrator shows it, all life would have been destroyed.

ILLUSTRATED BITS

X'MAS NUMBER

1d.

ENGLAND
100 YEARS HENCE!

EDITED BY ATHOL MAYHEW.

ILLUSTRATED BY FURNISS.

Alas, he was invariably pessimistic, with a caution bred by years of making experiments, 99 percent of which have been failures. Take Signor Marconi, for example. However hard the interviewer might try, the inventor would not state, not *positively* state, that he could despatch his wireless rays into hostile battleships and explode their magazines by means of induced sparks. Perhaps he raised enough doubts to worry the naval mind — perhaps he even delayed the fitting of naval vessels with wireless for some years — but as for himself, no, Signor Marconi would not commit himself.

Nor did the interviewer who called upon Mr J. Swan fare any better. 'I do not think,' declared the great pioneer of electricity, 'that electricity will be found advantageous for, say, cleaning the windows, or scrubbing the floors of our homes, as imaginative writers have suggested. Nor would I dare commit myself to the opinion that electricity will entirely supplant gas as an illuminant.' All he was being asked to do was commit himself to an *opinion* — the interviewer wasn't even trying to extract a promise — and yet his nerve failed him. Yet within a few years he had founded with Edison the great electrical firm which was to perpetuate his name as one of the great exploiters, as well as one of the great inventors, of electrical power!

The journalist, meanwhile, was far more sanguine. The same magazine, only two years later, published a story *Our Animated Flat* where it is taken for granted that every possible use of electricity will be exploited. 'Servants will become an extinct race. Everything from the hall door to your beds and stoves will work by machinery, and the whole house will look after itself.' A dream which has still to be fully realised.

Waiting for an accident

The scientist had grounds for caution. He knew that many an invention has to wait for the rest of the field to catch up. If it hadn't been for the accidental discovery of the radio valve — by a gentleman who happened to be looking for something quite different — wireless would still be nothing more than a highly cumbersome method of emergency signalling. Similarly, at the very time when Marconi himself was publishing his well-proved discoveries, experiments were in progress on the subject of talking along light waves — experiments which were not successful, and could not have been until the discovery of the laser in the 1960s.

Man's dreams of rapid travel, in particular, were hindered by many difficulties, and above all by the matter of the power unit. Powered flight became possible only with the perfection of the internal combustion engine. The scientist knew that something of the sort would have to be discovered before he could achieve success, and until then remained cautious and even pessimistic: the journalist, incautious and optimistic, discounted the difficulties which troubled the scientist, and declared cheerfully:

'There can be little doubt that the successful flying machine will be constructed on the principle of the flying bird. After all, Nature has shown us how to fly: it only remains for us to copy her methods.' How many flapping-winged aircraft have flapped their way to failure in pursuit of the same non-sequitur!

The future of surface transport was quite as uncertain. Here it was a matter of choosing between rival power units — steam, petrol, electricity. There is little doubt that electricity would have won if a satisfactory battery had been available. Mr Edison, for once less cautious than his colleagues, claimed to have invented a battery which would sell for only a few hundred dollars, would last fifteen years, and enable one to travel anywhere. This seems to be one of the very few of his claims which was never realised: or perhaps he was bought out by an oil firm. At last, after a further sixty and more years, it looks as if the final victory may lie with electricity, after the internal combustion engine has had the field to itself for half a century.

A moment's reflection

Well, but if the future remained cloudy on the technological side, what of the effect of progress on the world at large? By and large, mankind had great faith in the scientist: and certainly the scientist had great faith in himself. 'Will the world be better and happier in the new century?' asked the *Harmsworth Magazine* as the nineteenth century crumbled. 'To us it seems that the answer should be unquestionably in the affirmative. Scientific progress tends to moral advancement. A moment's reflection will show that aerial navigation, rapid transit, the electroscope (= television), will all tend to make crime and war more difficult, while improved social conditions will make them less attractive.'

Since the new century began we have had more than a moment in which to reflect, and there is little sign that crime and war have become more difficult or less attractive. And even at the time the scientist's faith was not shared by all: for the journalist, this time, had doubts. H. G. Wells published his *The Sleeper Awakes* early in the new century: it was a brilliantly prophetic vision of an age when scientific inventions had been perverted to serve the debasement of religion and the enslavement of most of the population. It was a theme which was to be taken up by many writers during the half-century to come: but then they, unlike Wells, had had more than a moment to reflect in. He alone seems to have seen that science presented mankind, not with the certainty of a better world, but with a choice between paths which led to the better or the worse. Sixty years later we are still as undecided as ever which to choose . . .

Wells' was a lone voice in those years, and *The Sleeper Awakes* was set in a very distant future. The short-term prospect, anyway, seemed encouraging. Thanks to science, a calmer and more spacious life could be foreseen. Our cities themselves could be made into cities of dreams, our homes like fairy tale palaces. With gay abandon they imagined the shape of the world to come, as it would be when the scientist stopped messing about in his laboratory and gave them the magic gifts they were all waiting for.

Yet their glimpses of futurity have all one curious fault in common. They could not conceive the whole scene. Whole walls might become television screens — splendid: but the sound came through earphones, or curious antique horns. The city streets might be bathed in light at night — magnificent: but the electric lamps were hung from balloons tethered by ropes. Television sets were adjusted by great spoked wheels like the steering wheels of trams. Elevators are crude, clumsy affairs like the ones which can still be marvelled at in ancient department stores. Aircraft had open cockpits and gleaming brass handrails. A uniformed commissionaire stood at the landing stage, controlling the crowd from plunging to the street, three hundred feet below, by a silken tasselled rope . . .

'One crowded hour of glorious life'

So mankind was to be happy, thanks to the scientist: he was to forget his criminal and warmongering tendencies and play with his new toys. But not, alas, for long . . .

Mr de Lapparent was reasonably cheerful. The world would last 4 million years, he predicted: by that time the land would all have been washed into the sea.

Lord Kelvin was not so happy. We only had 300 years before us: by then all the oxygen in the atmosphere will have been used up.

Sir William Crookes was distinctly bleak, predicting the end during the lifetime of many of his readers. By 1931, he calculated, there would not be enough food in the world for us all.

Mr Tesla was positively alarmist. Unless we were very careful, we might produce at any moment sparks capable of igniting the atmosphere. Strangely enough, considering that he was intelligent enough to be the pioneer who gave us the first practical method of making electricity on a large scale, he seems to have neglected the fact that Nature has, in the form of lightning, been giving us sparks far larger than anything man has been able to achieve. And, touch wood, no disasters of more than local extent have resulted.

In our own time, we have seen such fears raised about atomic power, even though the biggest explosion created by man is negligible compared with those regularly performed by Nature in the form of volcanoes.

out of the freezing sea will
erge the crawling sea
atures who have been hidden
so long in the depths. . . .

in 1900 the potential of Uranium remained unsuspected. Great things were hoped from Radium, on the other hand: a little research on it had already indicated that a great future might result if only more of the stuff could be discovered. 'To some humble miner, working with pick and shovel for his daily bread, may be reserved a discovery of the utmost moment to mankind. The possibilities of Radium are immense: at present we can only dimly guess at one tenth of what it can do.'

Ironically, the writer continues: 'Radium is always associated with Uranium. There are a good many deposits of pitchblend, the ore of Uranium, but though the latter is used for colouring glass and china there is no great demand for it. It would hardly pay to work over for Radium, without being able to dispose profitably of the Uranium Oxide. If a great demand were to rise for Uranium, the cost of Radium would be much reduced.' And so the supreme fuel source of the future was passed over!

In any case, even though salvation for mankind might lie in minerals extracted from the earth, there was always some clever calculator at hand who would compute how long it would be before the earth, honeycombed by reckless miners, would collapse in on itself and carry our civilisation with it. Better, they would suggest, to turn to the greatest source of power of all — the inexhaustible sun itself! Solar power — there was the fuel of the future: and one that would continue for ever and ever!

But would it? Again Wells shows himself the truest, most imaginative prophet, and it is fitting that at the end of this survey of visions and visionaries, it is his genius to which we give the final word. For Wells, the end of the world would come not in the lifetime of his contemporaries, nor in that of their close progeny. But it would come on that day, billions of years hence, when the heat of the sun dwindled to nought. Slowly the Earth will cover with ice: out of the freezing sea will emerge the crawling sea creatures who have been hidden for so long in the depths: and if the civilisation they discover bears a surprising re-semblance to Victorian England, that is Wells' illustrator's lack of imagination, not that of Wells himself.